D1154187

THE HOME UNIVERSITY LIBRARY
OF MODERN KNOWLEDGE

157

CHRISTIANITY

CHRISTIANITY

EDWYN BEVAN

LONDON
OXFORD UNIVERSITY PRESS
NEW YORK TORONTO

Oxford University Press, Amen House, London E.C.4

GLASGOW NEW YORK TORONTO MELBOURNE WELLINGTON
BOMBAY CALCUTTA MADRAS KARACHI KUALA LUMPUR
CAPE TOWN IBADAN NAIROBI ACCRA

First edition 1932
Reprinted in 1932, 1933, 1935,
1938, 1945, 1948, 1953, 1955, *and* 1959,

Printed in Great Britain by
The Camelot Press Ltd., London and Southampton

CONTENTS

CHAPTER I

ORIGINS

THERE was a time when all religion was narrowly tribal: each people had its own gods and modes of worship: it is still so to-day over considerable regions of the earth. But already in antiquity when great empires, like the Persian, embraced a multitude of peoples in their frame, a certain coalescence of religions took place. Nineteen hundred years ago all the countries round the Mediterranean were subject to the Roman Cæsar, and a great variety of religions had come to be included in the sphere of one government. The predominant culture of the Roman Empire was Greek: higher education everywhere in the Eastern provinces meant familiarity with Greek literature; Syrians and Egyptians ambitious of literary fame wrote in Greek; in Rome itself Greek was the language of a great part of the population, descendants of Greek immigrants and Greek slaves. In Roman Africa and the Western provinces the upper class spoke Latin, read Latin books and wrote in Latin, but Latin literature was itself largely modelled on Greek literature, and the ideas it embodied derived from the Greeks.

Thus it had come to pass that the conceptions current everywhere among men of literary education, from the Atlantic to the Euphrates, regarding the unseen Powers who ruled the world, were taken from the Greek tradition and shaped by the vivid stories told in old Greek poetry about gods and heroes. Underneath this literary stratum an enormous number of local cults went on: some of them had belonged originally to one particular people and had spread to other peoples of the Empire, such as the worship of the Egyptian goddess Isis, now adopted in various forms all over the Greek world, or the worship of the Phrygian Mother of the gods, coupled with Attis her beloved, which had got a footing even in Rome. Yet non-Greek cults tended to be more or less Hellenized: Isis and Attis retained their native names, but in many other cases the native deity was identified with a Greek deity and worshipped by educated people under a familiar Greek name. The ancient cults of the city of Rome went on, but they were now mainly an affair of quaint old ritual, with few ideas attaching to them except that of a certain magical potency for guarding the State or the family against mischance; the practice of them was confined to the ruling people, the Romans; it did not extend, as Greek mythology extended, in a Greek or a Latin dress, to the Empire as a whole.

There was little conflict or jealousy amongst all these religions. So long as a man took his part as a citizen in the public acts of worship and the festivities by which the gods of his particular city were honoured, he was quite free to associate himself in addition, if he liked, with a voluntary group worshipping Isis or Attis, or any other deity, Greek or foreign. Isis was not jealous if he worshipped Attis, nor Attis if he worshipped Isis as well. A cult obligatory all over the Empire was the worship addressed to the Genius of the Emperor or the Emperor himself. This worship had been established with local variations by the different communities of the Empire, following the precedent of the cults addressed to the Greek kings of Egypt and Syria after Alexander the Great, and the Roman authorities would now regard any refusal to perform the specified acts of adoration to the Emperor or to his Genius as punishable disloyalty.

To the easy tolerance of each other shown by all these religions one religion in the Roman Empire offered a striking contrast—the religion of the Jews. The Jews were now everywhere, a people to whom their numbers alone would have given importance. The Roman Empire was Jewish to a greater degree than the United States to-day. The Jews stood firm in their refusal to worship any Power except the One God who had created heaven and earth, the God who had chosen Israel as His peculiar people. The odd thing is that the Roman Government, which made a point of respecting national religions, exempted the Jews from the otherwise general obligation to perform acts of Cæsar-worship; they were allowed to pray *for* the Emperor instead of praying *to* him. The Jews by their apparent unsociableness aroused strong antipathy in the city-populations of the Empire, but at the same time they exerted a strange attraction. Each synagogue had attached to it a number of people, not Jews, in more or less close connexion, who found in the religion of the Most High God something which satisfied their souls better than any in the medley of pagan religions. Many more would have become full proselytes than actually did so, had it not been for the requirement of circumcision, a fearful deterrent to Greek men. Women, even of high rank, probably became proselytes in larger numbers. What were the special characteristics which distinguished this one religion from all the rest?

First, the One God whom the Jews worshipped was a Person whose being was manifested in righteous Will. The gods of the Greeks in the stage of naïve polytheism had been persons whose acts were acts of definite will, though very often of unrighteous will, but as the thoughts of the Greeks became more mature, and the many gods gave place to the idea of one Universal Power, common among educated people in the Roman Empire, the personal character faded; the Divine Power was conceived as something general and static, remote from the individual, rather an enveloping æther. The God of Israel had the Oneness and the universality of the Greek philosophic God, and at the same time the dynamic personality, the warmth and intimacy, which had belonged to the primitive gods.

Secondly, since will is expressed in actions, and actions are done in time, the time-process had a value for the Jews which it had not for the Greeks. It was the realization of a Divine Purpose, beginning in the unique " mighty act " of Creation, and proceeding through a series of unique " mighty acts " of God, to a final unique consummation, still future, the complete conquest of evil and the bringing in of a new world in which God would reign unopposed as King. To all forms of Greek thought the time-process was an eternal recurrence, leading nowhere. Plato and Aristotle had taught that human life on the earth would continue for ever, but that each human civilization sooner or later perished by some natural catastrophe, flood or fire or earthquake, and was succeeded by another one built up by the few survivors. The most popular philosophy, Stoicism, held that the whole universe, which had come into being by condensation out of the Divine Fire, would one day be resolved again into the Divine Fire, but that then, after a period, another universe, just like the present one, would be formed, run a precisely similar course, and be re-absorbed into the Fire, and so on, world after world, for ever. In such a universe, the wise man would be as little concerned as possible with time, or with anything which happened in time, and find peace in the contemplation of static timeless ideas. No other religion cherished a hope like that of Israel. No other religion, that is to say, in the Roman Empire, for outside the sphere of the Empire, Persian Zoroastrianism had an attitude to the time-process and a hope closely analogous to that of Israel. It is to-day an unsettled controversy how much the Jews borrowed from the Persians, how much the Persians from the Jews, and how much the resemblances between the two religions were due to independent parallel development.

Thirdly, this Purpose of God in history meant the existence of a Divine Community, a "People of God." The choice of this People had been one of God's "mighty acts," and a series of other "mighty acts," acts of deliverance or chastisement or teaching, marked the whole story of this Community throughout time. It was being trained by God in order that ultimately through it the knowledge of God might be transmitted to all mankind. And the kingdom of God to which Israel looked forward as the consummation of the time-process was a communal bliss, the ideal state of the People of God in peace and righteousness and joy.

Fourthly, these wonderful dealings of God with Israel were set forth in a sacred literature, a number of writings, some many centuries old, some quite recent. The books which were regarded as of especial authority we possess to-day collected together in the Old Testament, and we can see that, taken just as human literature, the

Old Testament was probably far above any other literature which existed in those countries, apart from Greek and Latin literature. Of course, the ancient literatures of the Nearer East have mostly perished, but we have recovered considerable fragments of the Egyptian, Babylonian and Assyrian literatures; their literary level is distinctly below that of the Old Testament. Thus a Greek drawn to the Synagogue came into contact with the one body of literature outside the classical tradition which could hold its own against the Hellenic. No doubt the diction of the "Septuagint" translation would seem to him unliterary, if not barbarous and grotesque, but some of the great quality of the original must have come through, and even where the Greek was unusual and obscure, it may have had for him the impressive strangeness of an oracle.

There was a large Jewish population, mostly poor, using Greek as their ordinary language, among the medley of nationalities in Rome. In A.D. 50 or thereabouts the Jewish synagogues in Rome were convulsed by a dissension which threatened a disturbance of public order. The contemporary Latin writers from whom Suetonius drew could not tell him precisely what it was all about: apparently someone called Chrestus (a Greek name meaning "good," "kindly") with his followers had made the trouble. Tacitus, describing events of A.D. 64, had more exact information. He gave the name rightly, not as Chrestus but as Christus, an odd-sounding name to Greeks, for *christos* in Greek meant "smeared"; to the Jews the name was profoundly significant, because a rite of smearing the head with oil corresponded in ancient Israel to our ceremony of coronation, and the *Christos* specially so called (in the language of Palestine, the *Messiah*) was the expected King who would establish the Kingdom of God on earth. Tacitus was probably ignorant of all that, but he could state that this Christus was a criminal who had been executed in Judea under Pontius Pilatus (procurator of Judea from A.D. 26 to 36). The people called after him *Christiani* formed a secret society which had spread from Palestine to Rome: they carried on most abominable rites behind closed doors. Tacitus does not specify the crimes laid to their charge, but we know from other sources that he meant orgies of promiscuous sexual intercourse and ritual cannibalism.

We must remember that the horror of such secret societies was fixed in the minds of the Romans by what they learnt as boys from their history books about the suppression of the secret Bacchic cult in 186 B.C. That too had crept into Rome from abroad and spread widely in the dark; in that too the votaries were said to indulge in promiscuous intercourse and bind themselves by oaths to commit horrible crimes: amongst other things, they were suspected of wanting to set the city on fire. How much of what was believed about the Bacchic society in 186 B.C. was true we shall never know:

evidently Rome, when the extent of this secret society was discovered, was in a wild panic, and we cannot rely much on stories current at such a moment. The State suppressed the cult with extreme rigour; numbers of its adherents were put to death. It established in the minds of the Romans the idea of a secret religion as something which might serve as a cover for licence and anti-social crime.

And here was the same thing all over again! The religion of the Christiani seemed to conform precisely to the type of secret religion which was a bugbear of the Roman mind. It was natural and right that the State should suppress it, as it had suppressed the Bacchic cult 250 years before, though Tacitus thought that the cruelties inflicted—men and women smeared with pitch and set fire to at night for the illumination of the Emperor's gardens—went too far. Nero declared that the Christiani had tried to set the city on fire. A friend of Tacitus, Gaius Plinius, when he was governor of Bithynia (about 112), had to execute the law on the Christiani of that province (now alarming in their numbers) and so conversed with members of the community, as Tacitus perhaps had never done. To his astonishment what Pliny learnt of their religion did not at all fit in with the type of secret society on which the popular idea of the Christiani had been formed. All they did, he wrote in his letter to Trajan, was to meet together on a particular day before daybreak, and sing a hymn to Christus as a god, and then bind themselves with an oath, not to commit any crime, but not to do just the kind of thing which ordinary Roman and Greek society considered wrong—theft, adultery, fraud, breach of trust. " After this, their custom is to depart; but they meet together again later on to take food, ordinary, harmless food"—not any cannibal banquet, such as popular belief attached to them. But, innocent as their practice might be, their obstinacy in asserting absurd beliefs, when he reasoned with them, sorely tried the patience of an amiable Roman gentleman: pig-headedness like that, he wrote, really did call down punishment. Probably some verses of a Roman poet, familiar to him from boyhood, never came to his mind—verses lauding the tenacious just man who holds fast to his conviction, though popular opinion be against him and despots threaten and the world itself falls to pieces.

We know better than Pliny did what those beliefs of the Christiani were. By this time the Christian community was quite distinct from the national Jewish community out of which it had sprung. The vast majority of the Christians throughout the Empire were of Gentile race with Hellenistic traditions. The old Jewish Synagogue and the new Christian Church regarded each other with vehement disapproval. Yet the fact remained that the Man after whom the Christians were called, whom they believed to be the supreme manifestation of the Divine Power behind phenomena, was a Jew.

The first Jewish disciples of Jesus had recognized him, while he was still a wandering preacher in Galilee, as the Anointed One, the Messiah, whom the people expected to come some day to overthrow evil and establish the Kingdom of Israel's God. But that the Messiah should suffer and die was an idea which before that time, so far as our evidence goes, had never occurred to any Jew—that the Messiah should undergo the death of crucifixion, which, according to the Jewish Law, entailed a curse, was for most Jews utterly monstrous. The disciples, following, we may believe, indications given by Jesus himself in his discourses, combined the figure of the Anointed King with another mysterious Figure shown, as it were in a vision, in one Old Testament writing—the figure of a Servant who suffers on behalf of the people, and by whose stripes the people is healed. Jesus was that Servant, as well as the Messiah. His death upon the cross was an offering of himself in sacrifice on behalf of men. But his death was not the end. There is sound historical reason for believing that his principal disciple, Simon, surnamed by Jesus *Kephā*, "Rock," Græcized as *Petros*, on the third day after the crucifixion, had an experience in which he believed that he saw his Lord alive, and that during the next few weeks or months numerous other disciples saw the Lord. After the appearances had ceased, or had become very rare, it was believed in the community that Jesus was "in heaven," "at the right hand of God," as the pictorial language in use expressed it, and we must remember that Jews 1900 years ago were as clear as anyone is to-day that God has not, in a literal sense, a right hand. But all the current expectation of a coming King who would overthrow the unrighteous powers of the world by irresistible supernatural might and reign gloriously over a redeemed humanity still held good. Only the disciples of Jesus believed that they knew now who that coming King would be: no imaginary figure, the actual Master whom they had heard and seen and handled. On a day, it was believed, not very distant, probably in the lifetime of many who had known him before the crucifixion, he would be seen again, and this time it would not be an appearance to a disciple here, or a little group of disciples there, but a blaze of glory which would light up the sky from end to end, "when the Lord Jesus shall be revealed from heaven with his mighty angels, in flaming fire taking vengeance on them that know not God," and calling together his own people into the eternal Kingdom of bliss.

That the disciples of Jesus had experiences in which they believed that they saw him alive after his death—so far historical evidence can take us. When we go on to ask whether this was a merely subjective experience, a kind of hallucination, or whether Jesus really was alive and manifested his presence to many of those who had known him, and when we ask further whether this manifestation involved the disappearance of his crucified body from the grave and its absorption into the new unearthly body, as the early stories of the Resurrection indicate, mere historical inquiry can yield no answer. Which hypothesis we adopt depends on considerations which go far beyond a calculation of ordinary historical probabilities.

For some forty years after the crucifixion—that is to say, till the destruction of Jerusalem by the Romans—the Jews who held these beliefs about Jesus formed a community in Palestine with its centre in Jerusalem, no longer in Galilee, speaking the Aramaic which was the ordinary language of Palestinian Jews and observing the Jewish Law, in unbroken connexion with the Jewish people as a whole. They were known as Nazoræans (*N'sōrayyā*); they themselves, in speaking of their community, perhaps (as Harnack conjectured) adopted an Old Testament word which denoted the "congregation" of Israel—*qahal*, or an Aramaic equivalent.[1] At first the Sadducean authorities made some ineffectual attempts to suppress them by imprisonment and scourging, since their belief implied that these authorities had been guilty of delivering up the Messiah to the Gentiles to be killed. Then, since there was nothing irregular in the Nazoræans' way of life, they were left pretty well alone, except at moments when

[1] Professor F. C. Burkitt, in a letter to the writer, says: "Harnack's 'construction' seems to me very shaky. . . . We don't know what term they used for the Christian Society."

something occurred to provoke a fresh burst of persecution.

The Nazoræans had some practices which distinguished them from ordinary Jews. One was baptism as a rite of admission to their particular group. The baptism of Gentiles admitted as proselytes to the community of Israel was probably already at this date an established custom amongst the Jews. Nazoræan baptism was almost certainly the carrying on of a practice begun in the circle which had gathered round John the Baptist, and with which Jesus himself, and his first disciples, had been connected, before Jesus struck out a new line of his own. It is an obscure question whether the community of John the Baptist still existed in Palestine side by side with the Nazoræan community in the years following the crucifixion. It is also doubtful whether in the circle round Jesus baptism had continued to be practised after Jesus had separated from the community of John: the evidence seems conflicting. According to one passage (John iv. 1, 2) Jesus himself did not baptize, though his disciples did under his direction, but there is nothing to confirm this in the Synoptic tradition. At any rate when the disciples of Jesus became organized as a distinct community in Jerusalem after the Resurrection, they seem to have continued the rite of baptism as a matter of course. It was affirmed, if not from the very beginning, at any rate before the generation of those who had known the Lord had passed away, that the command to baptize had been given by the Lord in one of his appearances after the Resurrection (Matthew xxviii. 19). But whilst the Nazoræans kept on this Johannine practice, they maintained that it had a new significance. They believed that a new Divine Power was working in the community which was actually the power and presence of the unseen Lord, the *ruach qodshā*, "Holy Spirit": it came upon members of the community as a force felt to be not themselves, sometimes driving them suddenly to ecstatic utterance, but habitually quickening in a strange way thoughts and feelings and language in those whom it "filled." The bestowal of this Divine power on men was specially connected with baptism in the name of Jesus; in many cases a manifestation of it followed immediately on baptism, though we are told of a case in which there was an interval, and the Holy Spirit was not conferred till the leaders of the community had laid their hands upon the new adherents, and of another case in which the Spirit fell spontaneously upon men before baptism. The Nazoræans insisted that in the original baptism of John this element had been wanting. "I indeed baptize with water," John was alleged himself to have declared, "but there cometh one after me who shall baptize with the Holy Spirit."

The other practice which distinguished the Nazoræan community was that of communal meals in which the bread broken and distributed was said to be the broken body of the Lord and the wine in the cup passed round was said to be his shed blood. A tradition in the community affirmed that at the last meal which Jesus had had with his disciples on the eve of the crucifixion he had so broken and distributed bread, calling it his body, and delivered the cup of wine to be passed round, calling it his blood. In recent times some people have doubted the truth of this tradition, but there is not a scrap of real historical evidence to discredit it. Of the two earliest records of it in writing, the first is by Paul, who knew personally members of the Nazoræan community and had at one time been in close conference for a fortnight with Peter, a participant in the Last Supper (Galatians i. 18); the other is by Mark whose association with Peter had been even more continuous and close. It is true that in the Gospel of Mark Jesus is not stated to have given his disciples the command to repeat his action as a memorial, and that Mark's account, taken by itself, would not authorize our asserting that Jesus himself instituted a rite.

Between the Jewish Nazoræan community at Jerusalem in the year A.D. 30 and the Greek Christian community upon which, at Rome in A.D. 64, the hand of the Imperial Government fell with such ferocity, intervened a history of great developments and changes. The epoch-making step had been taken within ten years of the crucifixion, when men who had been members of the Jerusalem community, but were now scattered in Hellenistic cities outside Palestine, began preaching Jesus to fellow-townsmen who were not Jews and admitting them by baptism to the community, called by the term which the Greek version of the Jewish scriptures used for the "congregation" of Israel, *ecclesia*. It was in Antioch that the name of Christiani was first given as a popular nickname to the followers of the new way. From about A.D. 40 the most signal part in this work of forming non-Jewish communities of believers in Jesus throughout the cities of the Empire was taken by Paul of Tarsus. Originally a Pharisee and a fiery persecutor at Jerusalem of the Nazoræans, he had an experience near Damascus in which he believed that he too saw Jesus and was addressed audibly by his voice: a few days later he joined the local Nazoræan community at Damascus, and became before long an itinerant preacher of the faith. By A.D. 60 almost every principal city of Asia Minor, Macedonia and Greece, had its *ecclesia*, composed of people who called themselves "Believers" or "the Brethren" but whom the world in general called "Christians." In Rome itself there was a Christian community before Paul arrived there in 59 or 60; for he was only one of those who carried the "Good News" to the Gentiles, if the most eminent.

It could not but be that the religion of these Christiani, whose antecedents were Greek and pagan, whose mother-tongue was Greek and whose ideas were largely drawn from the current Hellenism, had a somewhat different character from that of the old Nazoræan community in Palestine. To some extent their ideas may have been shaped by teaching which was peculiar to Paul. But there we touch the most crucial and difficult of all the questions regarding Christian origins : What elements were there in Pauline Christianity, or in Gentile Christianity generally, which had not been in the primitive Nazoræan faith ? The question is difficult because, while we have documents to show us the Christianity of the Gentile churches—most notably the letters of Paul himself—we have no document which emanates from the primitive Jerusalem community without having passed through a Gentile-Christian medium. All, therefore, that modern scholars say—sometimes very confidently—about the beliefs of the primitive community are purely conjectural reconstructions, guesses at what perhaps you can see behind our documents when you eliminate the supposed Pauline, or Gentile-Christian, accretions. This applies especially to the account given in our gospels of the words and actions of Jesus himself. It is now generally acknowledged that the Figure there presented is encompassed, even in our most primitive Gospel, St. Mark, by a halo of divinity.

Since Paul's letters are largely controversial, it is fairly easy to discover things in which he *differed* from the primitive Nazoræan community. But what one especially wants to know is how far the primitive community *agreed* with Paul. And that is very hard to say. It may be just the most important things which Paul had in common with the primitive community that he says least about in his letters, because they were taken for granted.

The first great controversial question which came up, as soon as there was a church of Gentile believers at all, was how far it was to be required of these Gentiles that they should observe the Jewish Law. The admission of Gentiles to the community was not, in itself, a difficulty from the point of view of the Jewish Nazoræans. The Synagogue itself admitted Gentiles, if they became proselytes and underwent circumcision. And to many, if not most of the Nazoræans, who still lived as good Jews, even as the Lord Jesus himself had unquestionably done up to the crucifixion, it seemed right that Gentiles admitted to the *qahal* should be circumcised and in other respects observe the Law given of old to Israel by God. The presidency of the Jerusalem community had fallen to a brother (according to Roman Catholic doctrine, a cousin) of Jesus, whose name of Ya'aqôb we curiously have transformed in English into James,[1] and even the Jews who did not believe in Jesus bore witness to the severe correctness of James's manner of life. It was Paul, the ex-Pharisee, who led the fight against the demand put from Jerusalem upon the Gentile churches. Peter, the chief of the Twelve, on the whole supported Paul, and James

[1] *Hebrew* Ya'aqôb, *Greek* Iakōbos, *Italian* Giacobbe, then Giacomo, *English* James.

himself agreed to the Gentile believers being liberated from the obligation to keep the Jewish Law, except in the matter of a few taboos (abstinence from eating blood and meat which had been sacrificed to idols). But other members of the Nazoræan community did not give way so easily, and their propaganda among the Gentile churches gave rise to strong and indignant protests from Paul. He claimed to have received direct from the risen Lord Jesus, whom he had seen, his commission as an "Apostle," which put him on a level with the original Twelve, and his claim to apostleship was admitted by Peter and James.

CHAPTER II

THE CHURCH AMONGST THE GENTILES

WHEN there were communities of Greek Christians, living in a way which made it impossible for Jews to eat with them, wholly separated from the Synagogue, the Gospel of Jesus had found an embodiment quite alien to the group which had gathered round Jesus in Palestine. This transition had been something which the original disciples can hardly have dreamt of, the production of a new society from the body of an older society by a birth momentous and difficult. The new society could set out, as the Gospel of Jesus in its older embodiment could never have done, to conquer the world. There is a common idea that the teaching of Jesus himself had been something broadly human, the assertion that all men without distinction are children of the One Father, and that Paul adulterated and spoilt this simple Gospel by vain fancies and doctrinal subtilties. The truth is that it was Paul who first declared expressly that men of all races and conditions were called without distinction to become sons of God, and that in the community animated by the Spirit of Jesus, there was "neither Greek nor Jew, barbarian, Scythian, bond nor free." It is impossible to find in the authentic words of Jesus himself any statement to the effect that the prerogative of Israel was to cease, or that Gentiles were to be admitted to the family of God on any other terms than their acceptance of the Mosaic Law. There are some sayings attributed to Jesus, which seem to imply the very opposite. Those most closely associated with Jesus up to the time of his death showed by their behaviour in the time which followed that they had never gathered from their Master's discourse any intention on his part to invite the adherence of uncircumcised Gentiles. It was an idea which seemed to them, when it presented itself, startling and wrong. Of course, for those who accept the Christian faith, these facts would not put Paul above Jesus. Christians recognize that it was not the purpose of the Lord, during his earthly Ministry, to explain in words all that his Person and his coming meant, and they believe that when Paul proclaimed the equality of Jew and Gentile before God, he was really being guided by the Spirit of the living Jesus in heaven. But most of those who charge Paul with adulterating the simple teaching of Jesus, do not accept the Christian faith, and for them the fact that Paul made this proclamation, and Jesus did not, is awkward.

Another element present in the teaching of Paul, but absent from the discourses of Jesus (if we allow the probability that the discourses put into his mouth in the Fourth Gospel are rather the expression of the faith of the Christian Church than sayings which Jesus himself ever uttered) is the explanation of the Person of Jesus as the Divine Being who has assumed humanity from love to men. Here again it is a confusion of thought to say that if the Christian Church makes an essential part of its Gospel something which is found in the teaching of Paul and is not found in the teaching of Jesus, that is to put Paul as a teacher above Jesus. For, according to the Christian faith, the chief significance of Jesus is not in what he taught, but in what he was and in what he did, and if he did not himself explain in words the significance of what he was and what he did, but left that to be explained by his servants, under the guidance of his Spirit, later on, when he was no longer present to the sight of men, that is obviously not to make the servant superior to his Lord. Those, however, who do not accept the Christian faith are generally disposed to see in this element of Paul's teaching something borrowed, perhaps unconsciously, from the pagan environment. Much in recent times has been made of certain " mystery religions " existing in the Græco-Roman Empire, ecstatic cults of a god who had been slain and had been restored to life, Osiris or Dionysos or Attis or Thammuz, originally a personification of the vegetable life which died down in the winter or in the heat of the summer, and revived in the spring. It is further supposed that owing to the influence of such religions new ideas were imported, by Paul or by later leaders of Gentile Christianity, into the two rites which that Christianity inherited from the old Nazoræan community—baptism and the Lord's Supper. Baptism was now regarded as a rite which magically conferred a new supernatural life and in the Lord's Supper the bread and wine were regarded as actually the God, Jesus, whom the participants took into themselves. In itself, it is not unnatural, as has been said, that Gentiles who became Christians should bring with them some ideas from their old environment; indeed it was inevitable, from the mere fact that the Gentile churches talked Greek, that their thoughts about things should differ in some ways from the thoughts of the first Aramaic-speaking disciples. In regard, however, to these particular theories the case is not so simple as some people suppose. In the first place, no one has been able to point to any real parallel in pagan religion to the belief that the Divine Being had come down to suffer and die for love of men: this idea is quite absent from the myths of Osiris and Dionysos and Attis and Thammuz, and it is the essential thing in the Christian belief. In the second place, no one has been able to find any evidence that the idea of eating the god, which is no doubt found among primitive people, was still current in the Græco-Roman world of the first century, even if certain practices still kept up had originally had that meaning. We know, as a matter of fact, almost nothing about the inner life of the pagan mystery-associations and imaginative reconstructions of it to-day often import into it, without any warrant, features of the Christian eucharist, and then build theories on the resemblance. Again, in comparing Gentile Christianity with the belief of the primitive Jerusalem community, we are comparing it, as has been said, with something which is largely an unknown quantity. We know that the primitive community was troubled when Paul told Gentile converts that they need not keep the Law, but there is not a trace of Peter or James finding in Paul's teaching about Jesus anything which was strange and new. Paul never puts that forward as something he had to maintain against contradiction. We cannot, it is true, say whether in the primitive community the idea of re-birth was expressly connected with baptism or not, but it is clear that the idea of possession by the Holy Spirit was, and possession by the Holy Spirit was in practice not very different from re-birth. We cannot again say precisely what ideas were attached in the primitive community to the bread broken and the wine drunk at the communal meals, but whereas Paul, and Gentile Christianity after him, affirmed them to be the Body and the Blood of the Lord, it cannot reasonably be questioned that the tradition which described how the Lord, at the Last Supper, had called the bread his body and the wine his blood went back to the original Twelve.

Certain broad historical facts are beyond

controversy. One is that, whether or no the belief that the Divine Being had descended to die for love of men was a true belief or a delusion, it was the universal belief of the widely diffused society of Gentile Christians which confronted the Imperial authorities, a novel phenomenon in the world, in the latter part of the first century A.D. Another fact which cannot be denied is that this belief, whether true or false, has given ever since to all distinctive manifestations of the Christian spirit a certain quality which does not belong to moral virtue apart from the belief. For all efforts of the Christian to conform to the ideal, in control of his animal impulses or in service of his fellows, are the response to a Divine love which must leave his highest possible attainment hopelessly short of the debt he owes. The belief, in proportion as it has been genuinely held, has produced the greatest moral effort together with the greatest humility and sense of unworthiness in achievement. Nothing is obviously more mistaken than to regard such a belief as a theological dogma without immediate relation to emotion or practice. As a matter of mere psychological fact, the thought of the Cross, in the significance given to it by Paul, has counted for far more, as the mainspring, throughout nineteen centuries, of Christian devotion, of Christian service and self-sacrifice, than the Sermon on the Mount. What Jesus was and did, according to this belief, is greater and more wonderful than what he said.

But whatever differences there were between Gentile Christianity and the primitive Nazoræan community, the foundation of Gentile Christianity remained always the old Hebraic presuppositions. Firstly, for Christians, God was still the One God, a Person whose character was righteous Will, the Creator of the Universe and yet intimately near to each individual soul. It was common among the Jews to speak of God as "our Father in heaven": for the Christians the term had acquired a special meaning through their incorporation in Christ. The Aramaic word "Abba" (Father), which Jesus had used, was retained in the Greek-speaking churches as a cry of the heart.

Secondly, the time-process was still for the Christians the expression of a Divine purpose; it moved from the unique beginning, Creation, to the unique end, the final triumph of good over evil, and it was marked all along at successive points by unique "mighty acts" of Divine love and judgment. Like the primitive Nazoræan community—indeed like the writers of Jewish apocalypses—the Christians thought that the end was very near. They expected any day to see Jesus return on the clouds and all the Imperial strength and splendour of the pagan world melt to nothing at his glance. As time went on this expectation inevitably lost its vividness. But it is not true to say that the belief in the relative nearness of the Second Advent was generally given up, before the nineteenth century. Christians of later genera-

tions did not indeed, as a rule, count on the likelihood of its occurring in their own lifetime, but they commonly thought that the present world had not more than a few centuries at most to run; and it would probably be possible to find in every successive generation of Christians up to the present, some utterances to the effect, "These are evidently the last days"; in times of religious excitement, over and over again, throughout nineteen centuries, the expectation of the Lord's return as something immediate has revived.

Of course, it is true that, while Jews and Christians both saw in the time-process a succession of "mighty acts" of God, the particular mighty acts which Christians affirmed to have been wrought "in these last days," the Jews declared to be incompatible with the Divine nature. There was indeed a similitude in the old Hebrew books in which God's love for His people was represented as like that of a shepherd who goes forth to seek his lost and wandering sheep. "Behold I myself, even I, will search for my sheep, and will seek them out. As a shepherd seeketh out his flock in the day that he is among his sheep that are scattered abroad, so will I seek out my sheep; and I will deliver them out of all places whither they have been scattered in the cloudy and dark day." (Ezekiel xxxiv. 11, 12.) But that for the Jews was only poetical imagery. The Christians, on the other hand, affirmed that, just as in men love implied self-giving for the loved persons, self-humiliation, self-sacrifice, so God's love was such that He had actually and really, not in a figure, but in the person of the Being who was one with Himself, come into the dark and cloudy sphere of men's pain and sin, to seek, to serve, to suffer, to offer Himself to the uttermost in order that men might be drawn to Him and be saved from pain and sin and death. It would be a mistake to try to minimize the profound disagreement between Jews and Christians in regard to the validity of such a conception. But in spite of that disagreement it remains true that the Hebraic conception of the world-process as a unique one, marked by unique events of supreme religious significance, remained fundamental both for the Christian and for the Jewish view of human life. In the second century the Church came to express its distinctive beliefs in a stereotyped formula which a new member recited at his baptism, in a "creed." Sometimes one hears it said to-day that the Christian creeds show that Christianity had changed from an Hebraic faith into a Greek mystery-religion. Nothing can be further from the truth. The two chief Christian creeds consist for the most part of statements of belief that certain unique events took place, or are going to take place, at particular moments of the time-process. That is an Hebraic, not a Greek, attitude to the Universe. When we remember that the Græco-Roman world, as has been said, viewed the time-process as an eternal repetition leading nowhere, we can understand how a Gospel which told men that it was a process leading to a great goal came as something liberating and new. An eminent German philosopher of our own day, Heinrich Rickert, has indicated this as the main reason why people forsook their old religions for Christianity.[1] A man who got divine life in a Greek mystery-religion believed himself to have moved upwards individually into a higher sphere, but a man incorporated in the Christian community was brought into a stream of dynamic *communal* life, going on through time, in which he was carried onwards to a transcendent future consummation.

The third characteristic we noted of Hebrew religion was the belief that the Divine Purpose in the time-process was embodied in a special community, an elect "People of God," whose life went through the ages and whose ultimate perfection would be the consummation which gave the process its meaning and worth. Here again, the Christians carried on the Jewish belief, although they disagreed with the Jews on the question what actual community was the People of God in the present state of the world. For the Christians it was no longer the community of old Israel, constituted by physical descent and the incorporation of proselytes who kept the Mosaic Law; it was the new "congregation" (*ecclesia*), the "new Israel," whose members were drawn from any race of man

[1] Quoted in F. von Hügel, *Essays and Addresses*, Second Series (Dent, 1926), pp. 30, 31.

without distinction, and whose Law was the new "Law of Christ." The word *ecclesia* English usage renders by the word "Church," derived from quite a different Greek word[1]: this somewhat obscures the fact that *ecclesia* was the Septuagint translation of the Hebrew *qahal*. On the question who the people of God had been up to the coming of Jesus, Jews and Christians were agreed; but now there were two rival communities each claiming, against the other, to be the true continuation of the Old Testament Israel.

The Christian Church was the continuation of Israel, but the continuation, according to Christian belief, with a great difference. Gentile Christianity retained the belief of the primitive Nazoræan community, that the Holy Spirit entered into those united to the Church by faith and baptism. In some of the Gentile churches of the first century, there were ecstatic outbreaks, regarded as manifestations of this indwelling of the Spirit, especially "glossolalia," that is, unintelligible utterance believed to be an unknown language, possibly a language of angels. Paul, while he did not question that the power behind such utterance might be really the Spirit of God, while he told his converts indeed that he himself "spoke with tongues"

[1] That "church" is derived from the Greek *kyriakon* is the ordinary view: recently, however, it has been maintained that it is really derived from a Celtic word *cruc* (Latin *circus*) used of the round sacred barrows of the heathen Celts. A. Hadrian Allcroft, *The Circle and the Cross*, Macmillan, 1927.

more than any of them, on the whole tried to divert their interest to the "more excellent" manifestations of the Spirit, "love, joy, peace, longsuffering, kindness, goodness, faithfulness, meekness, self-control" (Galatians v. 22), especially love, or, as the word is sometimes translated, charity (1 Corinthians xiii).

But if this Spirit, penetrating and controlling all the members of the *ecclesia*, was so closely associated with the person of the Lord Jesus that where the Spirit was present Jesus was present, then the *ecclesia*, as a whole, formed a single organism, whose life and thoughts and activities were derived continuously from its one "Head," the Lord alive in the unseen world. Each individual Christian was, in a sense almost more than figurative, a "member of Christ." The Son of God was still here in the world, though after a different mode from that when he was seen as a man among men, belonging to a particular Jewish family: now, since the Resurrection, he was a diffused power of holiness, working in all the members of his extended "Body" throughout the world (Romans i. 4). There had been nothing like this in the old *ecclesia* of Israel: in this respect the Christian "Church" was not a continuation of anything, but a wholly new creation, whose birthday was the moment when the Spirit issuing from the Lord Jesus in heaven had first descended upon the group of disciples in Jerusalem.

The fourth characteristic of Judaism had been its possession of sacred and authoritative scriptures. Here the Christian Church continued Hebrew religion, not only by having scriptures, but by retaining the actual Jewish scriptures as its own. The only Christian Bible to start with, was the Greek "Septuagint" version of the Hebrew Old Testament. Together with the books recognized by the Synagogue as of Divine authority there circulated amongst the Christians a few books also, produced by Jews in the last two centuries preceding the Christian era, which in course of time were put by the Christian Church on the same level as the books of the Jewish Canon, these later books constituting what Protestants call "the Apocrypha," and including one work, at any rate, of high religious and literary value, the "Book of Wisdom." The Christians agreed with the Jews in believing the Hebrew scriptures to have been inspired by God, but they claimed, against the Jews, that these scriptures now belonged to the Christian Church, the true continuation of Israel. It was a difficulty that the Jewish Scriptures included the Law, in which a mass of ceremonial observances were enjoined as commands of God. When Paul contended that Gentile believers were freed from the Law, he took the line that there had really been an obligation to observe these commands from the time of Moses to the coming of the Messiah, but that this obligation had ceased in the new community after the Messiah's sacrificial death. It had to be recognized that the Lord himself, before his death, had conformed to the written

Law as of Divine authority. Another writer, of the Pauline circle (the unknown author of the writing called, probably wrongly, the "Epistle to the Hebrews"), explains that the Jewish ceremonial Law had consisted of a mass of symbols, pointing forward to the realities manifested in Jesus and his community, and that the time of shadows had passed, when the substance was come. Now even the Sabbath Law, which was included in the Ten Commandments, was declared to be no longer of obligation for believers (Colossians ii. 16).[1] This view of the validity of the Jewish Law, as real, but temporary and now overpast, became the established one in the Christian Church. In the earlier part of the second century some Christian teachers held that God had never meant the ceremonial Law to be literally observed, and that it was merely the gross unspirituality of the Jews which caused them to misconstrue symbolical imagery and offer animal sacrifices. ("Epistle of Barnabas," "Letter to Diognetus.") Such a view, however, found no acceptance in the Church after the struggle with Gnosticism.

In days when only a few could themselves possess copies of the sacred books, it was by the reading and exposition of the Greek Old Testament at the communal meetings on the first day of each week—the "Lord's Day," called by

[1] In the fourth century when Saint Augustine discusses the Ten Commandments as binding upon Christians, he excepts the commandment about the Sabbath.

contemporary pagan astrology the " day of the Sun "—that the community became familiar with the Scriptures. But the sayings of the Lord could not be of inferior authority to those of any Old Testament writer, nor his doings and sufferings of less importance than any Old Testament narratives. Quite soon, therefore, after Gentile churches came into existence, the floating tradition of what the Lord had said and done, was put into writing by various Christian teachers, according to the amount and the forms of the tradition which had reached each compiler, in order that such writings might be read aloud, together with the Scriptures, in the assemblies or used for individual instruction. A large number of papyrus rolls must have been in circulation at first in the different local churches, containing various collections of the sayings and doings of the Lord. But it was natural that the writings used in the churches of greatest prestige tended to get copied for other churches, and so displace the old local compilations. In this way, by the end of the first century, three writings had come into wide use. One was our " Gospel according to Mark," originally, it is thought, the " Gospel " used by the church in Rome, declared by a credible tradition to have been compiled by John Mark from what he remembered of the oral teaching of Peter. The other two were our " Gospel according to Matthew," emanating perhaps from Antioch,[1]

[1] Foakes Jackson and Lake, *Beginnings of Christianity* (Macmillan, 1920), I, pp. 329 and following.

and our "Gospel according to Luke," emanating, according to one tradition, from Achaea, that is, presumably, from Corinth. Both these two Gospels had incorporated the major part of St. Mark with slight verbal alterations, and had also incorporated large bits of an early and almost first-hand collection of the Discourses of the Lord, afterwards lost, which modern scholars refer to as Q (from the German word *Quelle*, "source"), and which was possibly translated from an Aramaic original drawn up by Matthew, one of the Twelve.

About the year A.D. 100, or soon afterwards, a fourth "Gospel" of a wholly different character, came into general circulation, emanating, it is generally believed, from Ephesus. Its author is given by tradition as John the Apostle, who is said to have lived at Ephesus in extreme old age. The opinion prevalent amongst scholars to-day is that the John of Ephesus was not John the Apostle, though someone who had really, as a lad, known Jesus in Jerusalem, and some scholars suppose that he had afterwards been closely associated with John the Apostle. If so, his Gospel would be to some extent derived from the memories of one of the Twelve.[1] But, of course, the Fourth Gospel is

[1] Whether the "disciple whom Jesus loved," referred to in the Gospel, was the author himself or John the Apostle is a moot point. A note attached to the end of the Gospel (John xxi. 24) states that the disciple was the author of the book, "and we know that his testimony is true." Unfortunately there is nothing to show who the "we" are, here appearing

still one of the problems of early Christianity. By the middle of the second century these four writings had got an authority in the churches of Asia Minor and the West which left all other collections of the words and sayings of Jesus behind.

Another kind of document read at communal assemblies might be a letter addressed to the local church from an eminent teacher belonging to some other church or itinerant and unattached. We have one such writing in what is called the "First Epistle of St. Clement," a letter written about A.D. 96 from the church in Rome to the church in Corinth. Paul maintained a correspondence with a large number of churches. Sometimes a letter sent to one church was a circular intended to be passed on to others (Paul's "Epistle to the Ephesians"). But even if it was not a circular letter, a letter coming from a teacher or a church of great authority would interest Christians generally, and so get copied and circulated and read, long after the original occasion of its dispatch had passed by,

in contradistinction to "his," or who appended this note. The elders of the church at Ephesus? Some particular group of Christians from whom the Johannine literature proceeded? Some scribe who later on (perhaps far away from Ephesus) made the copy of the Gospel from which our manuscripts are derived? Or can it have been the author himself who by a curious grammatical anomaly uses, in speaking of himself, both the first person and the third person in the same clause? In the absence of information regarding the author of the note, it is obviously impossible to know how much authority belongs to it.

in churches other than that to which it had first come. Several of Paul's letters in this way obtained a wide and enduring circulation amongst Gentile Christians.

Some of these Christian writings, read in Christian assemblies together with the Jewish Scriptures, afterwards obtained a place in the New Testament; some did not. The "Epistle of Clement" did not, though the almost contemporary "Epistle to the Hebrews" and the later "Gospel according to John" did. In the earlier part of the second century there was not yet any particular collection of Christian books recognized generally as Divinely inspired with a clear line drawn between the books in the Canon and books outside. Christians during the first four or five generations of the Church had not yet the "New Testament," in contrast with which the Church's original Bible came to be described as the "Old Testament." What in time made it important to have a clearly marked Canon of Christian authoritative writings was that there were writings in circulation which claimed apostolic authority and which were brought forward to support views recognized by the churches generally to be heretical.

CHAPTER III

THE PAGAN WORLD AND THE CHURCH

It was a society of such character, embodied in little communities throughout the cities of the Empire, that the Imperial authorities from the middle of the first century onwards had to deal with. The attitude of the society to the Empire, so long as the Empire would let it alone, was one of acquiescence, and even respect. It is quite false to represent early Christianity as a movement animated by "class-hatred" of the powers that be, on account of the social and economic disadvantages of the "proletariat." No doubt the Church included numbers of slaves, but, even in regard to these, the analogy of modern proletarians or of negro slaves would be misleading. A great deal of the higher intellectual work in the Roman Empire was done by slaves and ex-slaves, as secretaries, teachers, managers, and in the matter of education many a Greek slave was superior to his Roman master. Probably the Church drew the bulk of its adherents from small tradesmen and handicraftsmen, an analogy of the respectable, law-abiding class from which the Nonconformist communities in England draw most of their adherents.

It included a few people of high social rank, and, among these few, some very high indeed. Before the first century was out, the consular Titus Flavius Clemens, a cousin of the Emperor, whose sons had been as children designated heirs to the throne, became a Christian. The tone of early Christian literature is as unlike as possible to that of literature inspired by proletarian revolt. In the "Revelation of St. John" (probably about A.D. 95) we have indeed fierce denunciation of the Imperial power, as Satanic, and exultation at the prospect of the destruction of "Babylon," but that writing, belonging to a moment when the State authorities had just shed the blood of the saints, is not typical of Christian literature as a whole. The "Epistle of Clement" (written only a year or two later) is much more so, with its careful-stepping, correct gravity. Respect for authority as such is a characteristic note in this literature; the wild men who "speak evil of dignities" are a horror to it. Clement describes with admiration, as a model for Christians, the ordered discipline of the Roman army. Jesus had declared that to Cæsar should be rendered the things that are Cæsar's: Paul had told the Christians at Rome to obey the State authorities, as holding their office by providential appointment; prayer was regularly offered for the Emperor in Christian assemblies. No doubt men who were drawn to Christianity had a feeling that the world, as a whole, was dissatisfying and full of evil, and they looked forward with intense desire to the day when the Lord would appear and bring in a new heaven and a new earth. But that kind of religious dissatisfaction does not go particularly with the poor man's impatience of his social and economic inferiority. In fact the poor man's pressing concern for his worldly circumstances may even exclude the other kind of dissatisfaction. Spiritual dissatisfaction is more often felt by those for whom anxiety about daily bread is lifted, very often by those who have all the good things of life, and find them vanity.

In 64 in Rome Christians were for the first time, so far as we know, harassed and killed by the Government as malefactors. After that they were commonly regarded as malefactors, people upon whom any magistrate might inflict punishment, whenever he chose. Whether any law had been formally promulgated which made the existence of Christians illegal, or whether magistrates took measures against a society regarded as dangerous to the State, in virtue of their office, without any special legislation being required, is a question still debated on our fragmentary evidence.[1] But the odd thing in the whole story of the relations between the Empire and the early Church is that the Government, holding of the Christians the opinion which it did, persecuted them so little. No doubt Christians suffered continually from annoyances

[1] For the view that under Nero the existence of Christians was made illegal by formal law or Imperial edict, see C. Callewaert, *Revue d'histoire ecclésiastique* for 1901, pp. 771–97, contributions to the same periodical, 1902.

of one kind or another inflicted by their pagan neighbours, but Government measures of sanguinary repression were spasmodic and local. The persecution of A.D. 64 was perhaps confined to Rome, and the later persecutions till 303 were occasioned, in this or the other city or region of Gaul or Africa or Asia Minor, by some local incident, such as a popular outcry which caused the Governor or Prefect on the spot to let the sword, always suspended over the heads of Christians, fall. It was not till the year A.D. 303 that Diocletian instituted a general and systematic effort to exterminate Christianity over the greater part of the Empire, when it was far too late. This curious vacillation on the part of the Roman Government, striking now and again with atrocious violence, and then for long periods letting the Christian community grow unchecked, suggests that the Government was really puzzled what line to follow, when confronted with the new and mysterious phenomenon.

Why should the Government have persecuted the Christians at all? There were cults of pagan deities with secret rites all over the Empire, which the Government never thought of vexing. It was because the Church, in taking over from Israel the worship of Israel's God, had taken over Israel's intransigence. Just as the Jews refused stubbornly to offer worship to any god save the One Creator, so did the new Israel, the Church. The trouble arose really on one point: the Christians, like the

Jews, refused to offer incense to the Genius of the Emperor. But the Jews were dispensed from the obligation, because their religion seemed safely confined to the limits of a particular nation, and national religions Rome on principle respected. It was quite a different matter with a society which carried on propaganda to a far greater extent than the Jewish community had ever done, which set out to induce all the subjects of Cæsar, if it could, to refuse him worship. In a way Christianity was the aggressor; it had declared war on the whole fabric of polytheism and its war was carried forward everywhere, peacefully, invisibly, terrifyingly, so that a man might wake up any morning to find his wife or his son refuse to take part any longer in the familiar rites addressed to the old deities of the house. The adherents of the pagan mystery-religions did not object to participating in other pagan forms of worship: they did not object to throwing incense on the altar of the Emperor's Genius. All these cults together formed a happy family. If the Christian Church had been willing to join the family, like the cult of Isis or the cult of Mithras, it would not have been persecuted. Christians would rather die than offer worship to any god but God, and so the Empire felt, in an uneasy bewildered way, that it must fight them; it did not quite know how. Those other religions escaped the troubles which the intransigence of Christianity drew down upon it; yes, but the shrines of Isis and Mithras are now covered with the dust of over a thousand years.

The first law against Christians of which we know for certain was an edict of Septimius Severus about 200, which made the baptism of a new adherent a crime. But the persecution which followed lasted a very short time. Maximin the Thracian (235–8) issued an edict which attempted to cripple the Church by striking specially at its bishops and priests, but this persecution too was of short duration. A more severe persecution occurred under Decius (249–51), which lasted about a year. Then in 303 began the great attempt under Diocletian to exterminate Christianity by ruthless killing and torture. In the Eastern part of the Empire, the persecution went on till 311. But in the West the young soldier of Illyrian race, Constantine, who in July 306 was proclaimed at York Emperor for the Western provinces, was favourable to the Christians. When in 312 Constantine made himself master of Italy and Rome, he adopted the Cross combined with the monogram of Christ, as his Imperial standard (the *Labarum*). In 313, together with Licinius, who was his colleague in the Empire till 324, he promulgated the Edict of Milan, which established complete religious toleration, and restored to the Church all the property, churches and burying-grounds, which had been confiscated in the recent terrible years. From 324 till his death in 337, Constantine reigned as sole Emperor over the Roman world.

An incredible thing had come about. The Emperor professed himself a Christian! This was not quite what the first Christians had pictured. They had thought of Jesus returning on the clouds of heaven to destroy the Roman Empire. They had never pictured the Empire becoming Christian. Yet had anyone suggested such an idea to them, it would no doubt have seemed to them almost as miraculous as the other. But it happened.

It can hardly be doubted that the attraction of Christianity from the very beginning was social. It was not as a disembodied truth uttered into the air that the Christian "Good News" laid hold of men; it was through the corporate life of the little Christian societies in the cities of the ancient world. The life and spirit of these societies was indeed what it was because amongst them the Christian Good News was believed, but it was the life and spirit which gave the Good News its power. Men coming into contact with such a group felt an atmosphere unlike anything else. Each little group was a centre of attraction which drew men in from the surrounding world. In that way, probably, more than by the preaching of any few individuals, the Church grew.

What can we say, looking back, about the moral character of those first Christian societies? Two lines of argument have been taken in recent times, by those who think poorly of Christianity, to depreciate it. One line is to say that the standards of moral conduct held up by the early

Christians were so very *like* the standards recognized by the better sort of non-Christian Greeks and Romans that the claim of Christianity to have brought anything new of value into the world has no basis. The other line depreciates Christianity on the ground that its moral standards were so *unlike* those of the Greek world: they differed from the pagan Greek standards so much for the worse. Obviously, the two lines of argument are contradictory. It is the first line of argument only which could be used by people acquainted with ancient history; the second line of argument is simply ignorant. It is really true that the Christian conception of what was good conduct in a man's relation to his neighbours, and in his control of his sensual impulses, did not differ greatly from the conceptions upheld by the moralists of the Greek world. They too had made virtue consist in a man's mastery of his sensual impulses and in active benevolence to his fellows. If the Christians declared that a man should never seek to repay evil with evil, so Plato had said 400 years before. If Christians said that a man who receives a blow should not strike back in anger, so the Stoics said too. The kinds of conduct which pagan standards characterized as vicious—theft, fraud, murder, adultery, selfishness—were for the Christians as well the outstanding types of sin. The Stoics, too, had asserted that every man, in virtue of his humanity, was a child of God, and should be treated as such—even the slave.

"All men alike," wrote Dio Chrysostom in the second century, "have been created honourable by the Author of their being; all bear the same signs and symbols of their just claim to honour; all have Reason and feel the difference between the lovely and the base." He was protesting against the forcible prostitution of slaves.

Those who attack Christianity as having brought in a new conception of morals, contrasting unfavourably with that of the pagan Greek world, are usually thinking specially of the Christian rule in regard to sexual relations. The Christian societies regarded as the only legitimate sexual intercourse that between one man and one woman in legal marriage, the remarriage of either party during the life of the other, in the event of a separation, being probably regarded as adultery.[1] Against this it is supposed that pagan Greek society had a much freer, and a much better, view of sexual relations, regarding as blameless, or even as good, much which Christian society called fornication. The idea that ancient Greek culture was one which sanctioned sexual indulgence is not so common amongst classical scholars as it is amongst essayists and journalists, who take

[1] It is a debated question whether the New Testament does or does not sanction the divorce of a wife and the re-marriage of the husband in the event of the wife's infidelity. See on the one side R. H. Charles, *The Teaching of the New Testament on Divorce* (1921), *Divorce and the Roman Doctrine of Nullity* (1927), and on the other side, G. H. Box, *Divorce in the New Testament* (1921).

a modern literary mirage for truth. Of course, in practice, sexual indulgence (natural and unnatural) was thought very lightly of in ancient pagan society, but to make a cult of physical passion, to caress it with poetic sentiment, to talk tall about it, as about something which a man who is going to get the best out of life should seriously cultivate, that is anything but a return to ancient Hellenism; it is the fashion of a modern literary clique. The ancient Greek and Roman attitude was quite different. Sexual intercourse had no glamour: it was a low undignified act, man descending to the animal level, about which gross jokes were habitually made, as in the old Attic Comedy, or in indecent ludicrous images familiar to the eye. At the same time the ordinary run of men expected that their fellows would sometimes decline to such gratifications, and if they did, well, well, it would be absurd to make much of it, so long as the main part of men's lives was directed to more worthy ends. "It is pleasant to play the fool in season," only it should not be out of season. Men who wrote erotic verse were apt to excuse themselves by saying, as the younger Pliny did, that it was a mere fanciful amusement, and did not represent their view of things in real life. Marriage was a civic arrangement for a utilitarian purpose, the "procreation of legitimate issue," as the Greek formula ran. No doubt it was desirable that the man and woman so associated should form a rational human friendship; society admired the wife who was faithful and devoted to her husband and minded the house, but no romance attached to the physical relation. Those who followed the more earnest philosophies saw sexual passion as something almost wholly evil, one of the great wrecking forces in human life. The wise man might do his part as a citizen in procreating legitimate children, but he would, as far as possible, keep passion sternly suppressed. There is a remarkable passage in Plato, in which he meets the objection of the ordinary man, that the ideal of continence asked too much of human nature. Plato names a number of well-known athletes who, in order to attain the utmost bodily fitness, were reputed to have lived lives of absolute chastity. "*They* steeled themselves to abstain from that which the multitude reckons happiness, for the sake of a victory in wrestling, running, and suchlike contests, and shall our young men be unable to practise self-control for the sake of a far nobler victory?" (*Laws* 840).[1] Epicurus, the philosopher who made man's wisdom consist in the pursuit of temperate pleasure, left amongst his sayings one which might seem to have come from a Christian monk: "Nobody was ever the better for the carnal act, and a man may be thankful if he was not definitely the worse." The saintly Stoic, Musonius, a contemporary

[1] Compare St. Paul's, "Every man that striveth for the mastery (in the games) is temperate in all things. Now they do it to obtain a corruptible crown, but we an incorruptible" (1 Corinthians ix. 25).

of St. Paul, lays down rules for sexual relations which correspond closely with the Christian ones—all intercourse outside regular wedlock to be stamped as evil. Musonius indeed goes further in one way than the Christian Church as a whole has gone, though some Christian Fathers agreed with him: even in marriage there should be no intercourse except definitely for the procreation of children.

The ideal of chastity which Christianity put before the ancient Græco-Roman world was thus not different from that which the world recognized as the ideal already. Only now what had been an ideal had become actual in a remarkable number of men and women—and those not a philosophic *élite*, but a miscellaneous multitude drawn from all the common walks of life. When St. Augustine wants to set forth the special thing which distinguishes Christianity on the moral side from the old paganism, he does not claim that Christianity has a wholly new standard, he claims that the ideal once considered attainable by only a few philosophers is now attained by innumerable ordinary men (*De Vera Religione*, III, 5). And if this testimony is suspect, as coming from a Christian, there is the testimony of a pagan medical writer in the second century:

"We have seen in our own time those people who are called Christiani draw their faith from fables. Yet these people sometimes act in the same way as genuine philosophers do. Their contempt of death we can all see plain enough: also how through a certain kind of modesty they abstain from sexual pleasure. Indeed there are amongst them men and women who have never during their whole lives known the carnal act; nay, there are some who, in ruling and mastering their impulses and in their zeal for virtue, are not a whit behind real philosophers" (Galen, passage preserved only in an Arabic translation; a Latin translation from the Arabic is given in Harnack, *Expansion of Christianity*, 1, p. 266).

While, however, the best Greek paganism and Christianity agreed in condemning sexual relations outside the marriage state, and in sanctioning them within that state, Christianity invested the marriage state with a divine significance and sanctity it had never had for the Greeks and Romans. The love between husband and wife, the tenderness and care arising from the bodily communion which made each feel that the other was a part of himself, was a "great mystery," which means a great symbol: through it men could understand better the love and care of the Lord in heaven for his Body on earth (Ephesians v. 22–33). This was something new. The beliefs which Christians held about the Reality encompassing the life of man shed a light upon the relations within that life which gave them a new value.

It is true that later on the idea that sexual relations were essentially unclean, even in marriage, penetrated, as we shall see, into the Christian Church from its environment. It is also true that St. Paul sometimes advised men to remain, like himself, unmarried. But the context shows that this was not because he regarded marriage as in itself an unholy state, but because the moment was for him one of crisis ; he expected the whole earthly order of things soon to come to an end, and it was better for a man to avoid unnecessary commitments, and concentrate upon the Lord's cause, provided always that this renunciation did not produce a physical strain which would hamper him worse than marriage (1 Corinthians vii). So might a man speak in the crisis of a great national or social struggle. The only appearance which the idea that marriage is essentially a declension makes in the New Testament is in one of the latest documents where the idea is denounced as a doctrine of evil spirits (1 Timothy iv. 3), unless indeed Dr. R. H. Charles was right in detecting an intrusion of it in Revelation xiv. 4 ; but Dr. Charles's view of that passage is open to question. It must be remembered that the ethical ideas of the first Christians, so far as they were not shaped either by recognized moral ideas in the Greek world, or by the recorded words of Jesus, were shaped by the Old Testament, in which family life is given high value, and the idea that there is any special virtue in celibacy is utterly remote.

It is a mistake to suppose that the distinctive thing about Christianity was that it set before men a new code of conduct. The distinctive thing was an *euangelion,* a new *Announcement* of what God was, of what God had done and would do, not a new commandment. It is true that in the light of the Announcement the old commandment of love had become wonderfully new in depth and energy, had been given a new motive; yet the new commandment of the Christian Church was at the same time, to use the phrase of an early Christian writing, the old commandment which men had had from the beginning.

CHAPTER IV

INTERNAL CONSOLIDATION DURING FIRST THREE CENTURIES

CHRISTIANITY from the very beginning had in it two strains which might seem contradictory, which have in fact often led to conflict in the history of the Church, but which were both necessary to the life of the Body. There was the note of obedience to authority, and there was the note of free individual action and utterance according to the impulse of the Spirit. This latter was very strongly marked in the primitive communities, when "prophets" were common, who in the Christian assemblies broke into prayer or exhortation or praise, sometimes in unintelligible "tongues," as the Spirit impelled them at the moment. But it is a mistake to overlook the other note which was there also from the beginning. The relation of his disciples to Jesus was to One who was Master and Lord, and the New Testament shows us the leaders of the community, appointed by the Lord during his earthly life or, in the case of Paul, appointed by the Lord from heaven, exercising, after the bodily presence of Jesus was withdrawn, an authority in his name, which often looks autocratic. The epistles also show us in the local communities persons who direct and govern, and whom the other members of the community are enjoined to obey. How did these two strains work together—the authority of apostle and ruler and the "charismatic" freedom? That is very hard, on our scanty data, to say. When we see clearer, in the second century, into the internal government of the churches, we find everywhere, with perhaps the exception of Egypt, a single president at the head of each local community, called an *episcopos*, a Greek word for "overseer" which has come to be Anglicized as "bishop." He is assisted by a council of men called *presbyteroi*, "elders," Anglicized as "priests,"[1] and an inferior order of *diaconoi*, "servants," Anglicized as "deacons." By the practice of the second century, vacancies in these orders were filled only by transmission of office through the laying on of a bishop's hands, though the man whom the bishop ordained in this way had normally been elected or approved by the local community as a whole. All this is universally admitted; the great controversy regards the obscure interval which separates the Church of the second century from the days of the Apostles. For Catholics it is a matter of faith that the system of the second century goes back in essentials to Jesus himself,

[1] All that is meant to be asserted here is that the English word "priest" is a shortened form of the Greek *presbyteros*. Whether the presbyters of the early Church were "priests" in the Catholic sense has, of course, been a matter of immense dispute.

and had obtained ever since there was a Church there at all: all bishops derived their authority by transmission from bishops ordained by one of the Twelve or by St. Paul. This cannot be proved from the New Testament and other Christian documents of the first century. But the data are so fragmentary that any theory of the constitution of the primitive Church has to fill in large gaps by conjecture. And if the literary data do not prove the Catholic theory, they are capable of being made, on certain suppositions, to square with it. Those, however, who form their theories on the documentary data of the first century alone, apart from Catholic belief, practically all come to the conclusion that the Catholic system of the second century was not original, but a development of the third and fourth generations.

Some changes between the days of Paul and sixty years later are unquestionable. In the first century there is no indication of a single "overseer" presiding over a community, except at Jerusalem, where James, the Lord's brother, in A.D. 56 seems to hold a position similar to that of a bishop later on. Elsewhere those directing the several communities are always spoken of in the plural, as *episcopoi* or presbyters, the two terms being apparently, at this time, synonymous. In some cases these local directors are said to be appointed by Paul, or persons instructed by Paul, but we are never told that all presbyter-bishops were ordained by Apostles. Nor are we ever told how new presbyters or bishops were to be instituted, as the original ones died off. That is one of the things which makes all attempts to reconstitute a church order precisely similar to that of the New Testament, without going beyond the New Testament, inevitably futile. If you leave out presbyter-bishops, you leave out an essential part of the New Testament scheme; if you institute presbyter-bishops, you go beyond the New Testament in your mode of appointing them. It is as if you set out to build a bridge on incomplete specifications, binding yourself beforehand not to go beyond the specifications. It seems probable, as a matter of fact, that there was considerable variety between the arrangements in one local church and those in another—no uniform system at the beginning.

Again, sixty years after the death of Paul the "prophets" who played so prominent a part in the first century have disappeared. The weekly worship of the assemblies is now conducted by bishops or presbyters with forms partly liturgically stereotyped, and the ordinary members no longer intervene with ecstatic utterance. Ignatius, however, tells us (about A.D. 115) that he himself, a bishop, was occasionally moved to abrupt outcries in the assembly under the influence of the Spirit.

It is quite plain that the strain of authoritative order in the Church has become much greater in proportion to that of charismatic freedom. This was, no doubt, to some extent a psychological necessity. The beginning of a new kind of life, for an individual or a society, is often accompanied by an excitement and disturbance which afterwards gives place to a calmer more regular habit. But, besides that, the growth of the Church in numbers and diffusion made the problem of holding together all the local churches as one society a much harder problem. There was really an immense danger lest these scattered bodies, surrounded by the great sea of paganism, with religious and theosophical notions of all kinds rife everywhere by the mixture of races and traditions, should be severally absorbed and lost. It must also be remembered what a corrective to aberrations which claimed to be charismatic had existed in the personal authority of Paul and others of the first leaders. Sixty years after the death of Paul there were no apostles alive any more, at the most a few old men who, as boys, had known people who had seen the Lord. Where was a substitute to be found for the authority which Paul had exercised?

The crisis which the Church went through in the second century was the struggle with Gnosticism. In the Greek-speaking world around there had been many people during recent generations speculating earnestly how the universe, and this curious thing in it, Man, had come about, and what the destiny of Man was after bodily death. All kinds of different theories were afloat, but most of the theories had certain ideas in common. One idea very widely diffused was that the soul of Man was something divine, belonging to a higher world, which had come to be imprisoned in a material body; the idea was held in one form by philosophers, Platonist or Stoic, in other forms by the votaries of different mystery-religions. With all there was a craving for salvation, in the sense of the deliverance of this divine element from bondage to the body and bodily passions and its reunion with the divine world to which it properly belonged. There were different theories, more or less imaginative, how the divine element had come to fall from its original home into matter. One of the ways by which men thought that reunion could be secured was by a *knowledge*, imparted to a privileged few, regarding the way of ascent through the environing spheres in spite of the malignant dæmons who tried to bar the doors. A Greek word for such knowledge was *gnōsis*.

When numbers of people, whose minds were filled with such ideas, were drawn to the Christian Church, it was inevitable that they should try to combine these ideas with the Christian faith, which did offer points of resemblance. No Christians could go on permanently without exercising their minds upon the problem how Christian doctrines about the human soul, and about the coming of the Divine Being from heaven in the Person of the Saviour into this lower world, were to be fitted with what they knew, or thought they knew, of the universe otherwise.

A favourite theory with modern theological

professors is that the first generation or two of Christians were so filled with exuberant enthusiasm that they never wanted to think out what Christian beliefs implied: it was only when enthusiasm cooled that Christians began to worry about the difference between true and false beliefs. This is the kind of schematization which is dear to professors, but is quite untrue to human nature. No Christians, even of the first generation, can have lived in a condition of such uninterrupted ferment that they never cared to think, or were quite indifferent to the incompatibility of one belief with another, so long as both were proclaimed by men in the state of Spirit-possession. There was evidently from the beginning, when Paul and other leaders were there to make authoritative pronouncements, a process of rejection and exclusion in the matter of ideas and beliefs, as well as a process of assimilation. It is true that certain ideas and modes of expression were tolerated in the earlier generations, which were afterwards excluded. This means that authoritative definition extended (whether to the advantage of Christianity or not), but it does not mean that there was ever a time when the leaders of the Church did not exercise their authority to some extent in the rejection and condemnation of beliefs.

Before the first century was out there were teachers in the Church who had modified the faith delivered to them within the community by ideas they brought in from the environment outside. The term "Gnostic" which some of these teachers used of themselves and their disciples was afterwards extended by their Christian opponents to cover all teaching of a similar character. The interest of all these would-be Christian Gnostics turned on three main connected things: (1) the explanation how the world, with this strange fall of a divine element into an alien sphere, came about; (2) the explanation of Jesus Christ, the Divine Being who had descended into the lower world to save the imprisoned divine element in man, and conduct it back to its proper home; and (3) the means by which this salvation of the divine element was to be accomplished.

With regard to the first point they made a great distinction between the lower sphere in which man was living and the heaven where the Supreme Unfathomable God dwelt with the series of Divine Beings which had emanated from him. This lower sphere was not a creation of the Supreme Good God, but of an inferior god, ignorant of the Supreme God or actively hostile to Him. It was this inferior god who had been the God of old Israel, and from whom the Old Testament, or parts of the Old Testament, had come. (There were Jewish, or pro-Jewish forms of Gnosticism, but Christian Gnosticism as a whole was strongly anti-Jewish.) One of the Divine Powers of the higher world had, by a fatal and sinful aberration, fallen into the lower world, and was now under the dominion of the inferior, ignorant or malignant, God. It was this fallen Divine Power which constituted the Divine element in men—or, according to some Gnostics, in a privileged class of men, other men belonging by their whole nature to the lower world.

With regard to the descent of "the Saviour" from the higher world to rescue the divine element and restore it to its proper home the would-be Christian Gnostics assimilated the story of his descent through the spheres to the account of the descent of the Soul given in current Greek Platonizing fancies. The "Saviour," they agreed, had been manifested in Jesus, but the Christian belief that the Son of God had come down to suffer and die for men was abhorrent to them: a Divine Being could not suffer. There were two ways of accounting for the story of the Passion. One was that the body of Jesus had not been real; it had been an appearance only, and all his sufferings had been an illusion, by which the spirit-rulers of this world had been deceived. Those who held this theory came to be called Docetists (from the word *dokein*, "to seem"). The other way was to distinguish the Divine Being who dwelt in Jesus from the man Jesus himself. The Divine Being had quitted the body of Jesus and re-ascended to heaven before the Passion, so that only the man suffered.

Thirdly, there were a number of different Gnostic theories how men could obtain salvation, that is, the liberation of the divine element within them. There were various kinds of sacraments and ritual processes according to the particular school of Gnosticism. In the lower forms of Gnosticism these sacraments might be obscene, because sexual reproduction, by which the imprisonment of the divine element in matter was continued, was a matter of great concern to all the Gnostics. The theories of some led them to extreme asceticism and abstinence from all carnal gratification ; the theories of others led them to extreme licence and very nasty contraceptive practices.

The later writings included in the New Testament show the leaders of the Church already alarmed at doctrines akin to second-century Gnosticism, penetrating into the community. The writer of 1 John denounces Docetic theories, which deny that "Jesus Christ has come in the flesh." But when the original leaders were all gone, when, in the second century, Gnostic teaching of one kind or another kept cropping up in the scattered churches, the peril of a complete dissolution of Christianity was extreme. The Church had as yet no New Testament to appeal to, though all the books which constitute our New Testament had probably been written by A.D. 110, with the exception of 2 Peter, and were in circulation, as separate books. Unfortunately many other writings were in circulation as well. The Gnostics too had their Gospels, which professed to record the teaching delivered by Jesus to his disciples. Who could say which writings gave the true doctrine ? The Gnostic writings also claimed to emanate from the original Apostles. Nor was it only a question of writings; the Gnostics commonly asserted that one or other of the original Apostles had delivered a more or less secret oral teaching to a privileged few, which had been passed on from man to man, and this esoteric tradition various Gnostic teachers claimed authority to impart.

In all this uncertainty there seemed one firm thing to hold by—the persons who held an authority derived, not secretly, but publicly and demonstrably, from teachers of the first generation. The "overseers" in the several communities had been chosen for their office, as trustworthy exponents of the true tradition, with the sanction, at any rate, of predecessors who had been chosen on the same ground. If there might be a doubt in regard to writings, when so many writings were garbled or fabricated, here was a chain of persons whose connexion could not be denied. They could say with authority which writings had been recognized as true from the days when some of the original leaders still survived, which writings contained strange doctrine. They could declare the faith as they had received it in the light of day.

If we read to-day the letters of Ignatius, Bishop of Antioch (martyred in Rome about 115), with their continued insistence on each local church obeying its bishop, they seem to strike a note very unlike that of the first-century documents included in our New Testament.

But the insistence becomes easy to understand when we think of the circumstances of the moment—the original Apostles with their personal authority no longer there, the authoritative New Testament not yet there, and Christian teaching not yet set firm in its later mould. If the scattered Church was to hold together, its members, like an army marching through an unknown land, everywhere must rally to their leaders. There was one church especially, whose constituted authorities might seem to guarantee continuity with the founders of Christianity, the church of the capital, Rome, the central church in constant communication with all the provinces, the church which had received teaching direct from both the great pillars of the first generation, Peter and Paul. It is the church in Rome, to which, in the thick of the fight with Gnosticism, Irenæus (a Greek of Asia Minor who had become Bishop of Lyons in Gaul) specially appeals as being witness to the true doctrine against those who falsely claim apostolic authority and adduce written gospels other than the now recognized four (about 185). Even for those who reject the theory of papal supremacy held by the Roman Church to-day, indeed for those who reject any theological theory of Apostolical Succession, the appeal of Irenæus to the community of Christians in the capital and its undeniable series of presidents is perfectly intelligible on the ordinary grounds of human testimony, at a time when the authenticity of any written document might be called in question and the transmission of doctrine from person to person was the fundamental ascertainable fact.

The necessity laid upon the Church of safeguarding its proper character against aberrations which claimed to be Christian led inevitably to a hardening of forms and a firmer drawing of outlines. Against the teachers of strange doctrine there stood in each community the one duly constituted bishop and the body of presbyters; against the unregulated individual utterance in worship which, claiming to be impelled by the Spirit, might lead the community off on false tracks, there were the prayers and praises spoken by the ordained leaders, now to some extent in fixed liturgical forms; against the formation of dissident eccentric groups, there was the rule that no eucharist was valid, unless performed by a bishop or, under his authority, by a presbyter. Nor is it fair to judge this hardening of outline by the situation of later times. When once the Christian Church had in essentials secured a firm consistence, there would be much less danger in the formation of groups which tried new ways in thought and practice; such freedom might be all to the good; but in the second century, when the Church as a whole was new and tentative, a multiplication of little groups following different prophets, without any authoritative centres, might have led to a complete break-up and disappearance of Christianity in the pagan sea.

In two other important respects we see this hardening of outline, besides the episcopal system of church-government, in the fixation of formularies by which members of the Church declared their belief, and in the marking out a particular set of books as authoritative standards of true doctrine.

With regard to the second point, by the end of the second century the bulk of our New Testament books were established as authoritative in all the Christian churches—the Four Gospels, Acts, the Epistles of Paul, 1 Peter and 1 John. There were still a few books on the line, accepted in one part of the Christian world and rejected in another—James, Jude, Hebrews, the Apocalypse of John ("Revelation"), 2 Peter, 2 and 3 John, the Apocalypse of Peter, the Epistle of Clement, the Epistle of Barnabas, the "Shepherd" of Hermas. Ultimately the first seven of these books obtained a place in the Canon, and the last four were excluded. The New Testament thus came into being informally, by the common practice of the churches in the first two or three centuries. The ground on which a book was accepted or rejected does not appear to have been any systematic inquiry whether it had really been written by the person to whom it was ascribed, but the consideration whether its teaching did or did not agree with the true doctrine. The fact, therefore, that a book was ultimately admitted into the Canon is poor evidence regarding its real authorship. The precise limits of the Canon were never fixed by the formal decision of an Œcumenical Council, though from the eighth century onwards one may speak of general agreement in the whole Church, both Roman and Orthodox, that the twenty-seven books which compose our New Testament were canonical, and those only. But at the time of the Reformation it was still open to a Christian to express doubts regarding a book of the New Testament without traversing any defined dogma of the Church. For the Roman Communion that state of things was ended by the Council of Trent (1552–63), which finally declared, with an authority regarded by Roman Catholics as infallible, that the twenty-seven books, and none others, constituted the inspired New Testament.

When the controversy with Gnosticism in the second century had led to an extrusion of the would-be Christian Gnostics from the Great Church, the travail of the Christian community in regard to what was really meant by the Christian affirmations was not ended. Controversy had quickened thought, and thought, as we have seen, was bound to be largely shaped by the tradition of the Greek schools. What indeed was the relation of the Christian faith to Greek philosophy? That was a burning question. There were Christians who took the line that the ancient pagan education was evil through and through; all the Christian had to do was to affirm, in the formulas now traditional, the articles of the creed, and not try to establish any relation between them and the ideas which educated Greeks had about the universe. Greek education was the only intellectual education known, and to take this line was to declare for a Church permanently uneducated. There were men of great influence in the community who took the other line. Their chief centre was Alexandria, where from Ptolemaic times the greatest library of the Greek world had existed with a kind of university under State patronage attached to it. In Alexandria there were Christians equal to any pagan in their grasp of Greek thought, and here in the latter part of the second century we find a "Catechetical" School established, in which teaching of the Christian faith was given in close association with Greek intellectual ideas. Two centuries before a similar attempt had been made in Alexandria by the Jew Philo to combine Judaism with Greek philosophy, and the works of Philo were one of the foundations upon which the Christian teachers of Alexandria now built. The first of the two great figures of this Alexandrine Christianity is Clement, who was perhaps an Athenian (born about 150, died about 215). There could be no question now of a teacher in communion with the Church taking up the Gnostic theories which had been definitely repudiated, but Clement held that large elements in Greek philosophic thought were true, and that a Christian who combined them with his faith was a more perfect, well-equipped Christian than an uneducated one who had his faith only, and the more perfect Christian he did not shrink from calling a "Gnostic." He loved his Plato as well as his New Testament, and declared that for the Greeks philosophy had been the tutor leading to Christ, as St. Paul said that the Law had been for the Jews.

Against pagan polytheism Clement wrote as energetically as any Christian teacher, but in regard to Greek ideas which seemed to him compatible with belief in One God he was readily receptive—a warm-hearted, rambling man, with a large, but somewhat woolly, mind and a poetic enthusiasm showing itself in an eloquence which his Greek readers would recognize to be of the proper literary quality. His successor, Origen (born about 185, died 253), greater as a thinker, greater as a scholar, though indifferent in his writing to literary beauty, was the principal moulder of thought all over the Christian world in succeeding generations. Yet though Origen kept very strictly within the four corners of the recognized creed, and was never tired of exposing the errors of the Gnostic teachers, he was able to combine with the creed a body of theories which the Church repudiated no less than it had done the Gnostic ones. He believed in reincarnation, and held that all souls, angels, men and devils, had originally existed in a state of absolute equality in heaven; from that state they had fallen individually to different levels, and in the course of successive lives might move up or down, but in the end, he thought, all of them, even Satan, would return to their original state. When the Decian persecution broke out in 250, Origen, then living in Palestine, held to the profession of his faith with exemplary heroism, and died from the effect of the tortures inflicted on him. He is one of the most attractive figures in early Christianity—the ascetic passion for knowledge which made him one of the most learned men of his time, and the modesty with which he habitually puts forward his peculiar beliefs, as those to which he had been individually led, contrasting signally with the fierce dogmatism of some Christian Fathers. He is conspicuous among the very few ancient Christian teachers to whom the idea of eternal punishment was repellent. Of course, in his voluminous works there was a great deal which subsequent Christian teachers felt they could appropriate, so that the actual influence of Origen in the shaping of Christian theology was immense. In the Christian society of the fourth century "all thinkers were under his influence" (Harnack). Yet those particular theories of his which the Church repudiated brought him later on into very bad odour and strong language was often used in denouncing him. It is to be noted that neither to Clement nor to Origen does the Catholic Church to-day give the title of "Saint."

CHAPTER V

CONTROVERSIES AND COUNCILS

Two kinds of question had come to agitate the Church in the third century. One kind concerned the standards and character of the Christian life. It was inevitable, if the Christian society was to maintain its peculiar quality, in the face of surrounding paganism, that certain kinds of conduct should disqualify from membership, and that persons so acting should be excluded from communion. But when the line had to be drawn, determining precisely what things disqualified, and what did not, various judgments were possible. A special problem was presented by those who under the stress of persecution had given way and offered pagan sacrifice. Were they to be received back, when the persecution was over, and so ultimately have the benefits of membership in the Body on cheap terms, whilst those who stood faithful had to endure torture? The Christian writer, Tertullian (160–245), expressed a view very widely held when he laid down that there were seven kinds of sin which entailed perpetual exclusion from the Church without possibility of re-admission—murder, idolatry, theft, apostasy, blasphemy, fornication and adultery. When Callistus, Bishop of Rome from 219 to 223, declared and pronounced to adulterers and fornicators, being penitent, the absolution and remission of their sins, many besides Tertullian were shocked. Callistus was attacked as lowering the whole tone of Christian society, though the Church as a whole in the end went with Callistus. Of course, all Christians acknowledged the readiness of God to receive into His community, to forgive freely, sinners however desperate and vile, from the world outside: all the filth of the past was washed away in the water of baptism: the question concerned those who had been cleansed, who had been admitted, whether, if they fell back into one of these seven kinds of sin, they could be cleansed a second time. There could be no second baptism. The stricter view seemed to find support in the anonymous Epistle to the Hebrews, which was commonly believed in Roman Africa, at the time of Tertullian, to have been written by St. Barnabas: "If we sin wilfully after that we have received the knowledge of the truth, there remaineth no more sacrifice for sins, but a certain fearful looking for of judgment and fiery indignation which shall devour the adversaries" (Hebrews x. 26, 27). There were some who agreed with Callistus that adulterers and fornicators might be received back if they gave proof of repentance, but took the severer view in regard to those who had given way under persecution. This was the case with the body of Christians, called after Novatian, who claimed to have been validly ordained Bishop of Rome in 251. They broke away from the main body of the Church, declaring that by the re-admission of the lapsed, that Church had forfeited its right to be considered the Divine Community, and they maintained a Church of their own which lasted on into the sixth, or perhaps even the seventh, century. They did not deny that the lapsed might secure God's forgiveness, but they asserted that the Church had no authority to re-admit them to communion.

The other kind of question which agitated the Church from the third to the seventh century was theological, what was the true doctrine about the Person of Jesus. It is obvious to us, looking back, that Christianity from the beginning was confronted by a difficult problem in theology with which, sooner or later, it would have to grapple systematically—a problem which has not lost its difficulty for the Christians of to-day. On the one hand the Christian Church took over from the Jewish community the contention, against ideas prevalent in the pagan world, that the Power ruling behind phenomena was personal and was One. That was something fundamental. On the other hand the Christians gave to a particular human Person a place which seemed the same as that given, in worship and devotion, to God. From the very beginning Christians must have been asked by Jews and Greeks: But what do you *mean* when you talk in this way about Jesus? At first, no doubt, different Christians gave different explanations in answer to such a question—explanations which did not all agree. The attempt to find a mode of expression which the Church as a whole could adopt, in order to state what Christians meant, caused a trouble which extended over six centuries in antiquity and is recrudescent in our own days. Those centuries were full of theological controversy—metaphysical phrases bandied to and fro about the nature of Jesus.

It was not till Christianity had become the religion of the Emperor that it was possible for representatives of the local churches throughout the world to meet together in Council in order to formulate the mind of the Church as a whole on controverted questions. Such a Council was called an *Œcumenical* Council, from the Greek word *oikūmenē*, "inhabited world." Before that time different bishops could take their own line in regard to controversies which emerged; to some extent by correspondence they could bring about concerted action over the area of the Græco-Roman world; the prestige of the great churches such as Rome, Alexandria and Ephesus, would tend to bring others into line; but the Church had no way of formally declaring its mind as a whole. Controversy with the Gnostics had necessarily brought different views as to the relation of Jesus to God into conflict. Already at the beginning of the third century some Christian teachers

(Noëtus and others) were interpreting the Oneness of God to mean that the distinction between the Father and the Son was simply a difference of presentation; there was no distinction within the Godhead itself; and they accused their opponents of having two Gods. Their opponents accused them of implying that God the Father suffered and died upon the Cross. Again, in the latter half of the third century Paul of Samosata, Bishop of Antioch, represented to us as a wealthy and worldly Broad-Churchman, secured the Oneness of God by definitely making Jesus *not* God; Jesus was a man who through the existence in him of some divine quality had been exalted to heaven.

After Christianity had become the religion of the Imperial court, the bishops from all parts of the world in which Christianity had been planted—or priests to represent them—were from time to time called together by the Emperor to an Œcumenical Council. There were seven such Councils before the disagreements between Latin (Western) and Greek (Eastern) Christians prevented the holding of any more councils recognized by the whole Church. The first Œcumenical Council was convoked by Constantine, and met in 325 at Nicæa (Isnik in Asia Minor). This was the most epoch-making. The other six were (2) the first Council of Constantinople (381), (3) the Council of Ephesus (431), (4) the Council of Chalcedon (451), (5) the second Council of Constantinople (553), (6) the third Council of Constantinople (680),

(7) the second Council of Nicæa (787). There have been since then throughout the Christian centuries a number of Councils (including the Vatican Council of 1870), which the Roman Church regards as Œcumenical, because the Roman Church believes itself to be the one legitimate Christian communion in the whole world; but these later councils were not attended by the representatives of the Greek "Orthodox" Churches, and are not regarded by those churches, nor by the Anglican Church, as having been really Œcumenical.

In all the seven Œcumenical Councils just enumerated, it was questions touching the nature of Jesus on which the assembled bishops had to declare the faith of the Church. The occasion of the first, the First Council of Nicæa, was the Arian controversy. A priest of the Greek Christian Church in Egypt, Arius (Areios) about the year 318 had put forward a fresh definition of the relation of Jesus to God. According to this, the Being called the Son was the highest of created beings, created by God before any other, but he was himself not God, and could be called God only by a figurative extension of the term. This Being had appeared as a man in Jesus, but just as the Son was not properly God, so Jesus had not properly been a Man; he had not really had a human nature, though he had a human body. Arius adduced a certain number of texts from Scripture in support of his theory, and a considerable fraction of the Christian priesthood rallied to it. His great opponent was another Egyptian Christian, Athanasius. The first Œcumenical Council had to give a judgment on this controversy, and it decided in favour of Athanasius. The Son was also God, " begotten," not created. The special term which now came into use to signify the doctrine for which Athanasius fought was *homo-usios*, " of the same substance ": the Son was not the Father, but he was *homo-usios* with the Father. Some Christians disliked the term because it was not found in the Scripture, but such an objection was obviously futile. The meaning of the scriptural phrases was precisely what was in dispute, and therefore, if any formula could be found to fix the sense in which fourth-century Christians understood them, it had to be a phrase taken from elsewhere.

If this movement in the Christian community to emphasize the deity of the Son had been simply due to a tendency amongst the followers of a wonderful man to raise him ever higher and higher till the ultimate extravagance of equality with God was reached, we might have expected that the decision at Nicæa would have left no more to do. The noteworthy thing is that Christians were no less concerned to assert the real humanity of Jesus against people who would volatilize that, in order to secure his divine nature, than they were to assert his deity. The first Council of Constantinople (381) condemned the view of Apollinarius, that in Jesus the Divine Logos (Word) took the place of a human soul. No: Jesus had not only a body like other men, but a human soul as well: he felt and perceived and thought in the way a man must do, as man. But, if Jesus was both God and Man, was it right to speak of things true of him in his human character as true of God? Could one, for instance, without impiety, call the mother of Jesus the Mother of God? Nestorius, Bishop of Constantinople, held that such a mode of speech was wrong: to-day Christians of the Reformed Churches would almost all agree with him: but in 431 the Council of Ephesus affirmed that the union of Divine and Human in Jesus was of a character to justify such phraseology. The doctrine of the two *natures* joined in the one *Person* was affirmed more explicitly at Chalcedon (451): the formula there adopted has been ever since the basic formula in the Catholic doctrine about Jesus. A considerable number of Christians, however, in the Greek East refused to bow to this decision, and split away from the main body of the Church. They are described in Church History as "Monophysites" ("One-nature people") because they maintained that the Divine and Human in Jesus did not form two distinguishable natures, but coalesced to form one single nature. In Syria and Egypt especially the Monophysite view found favour. To-day the ancient Armenian Church, the Copts, the Abyssinians and the so-called "Syrian" Christians of South India are Monophysites, and are not in communion with the Greek Orthodox

Churches. Another name for Monophysites is Jacobites. The Second Council of Constantinople (553) added nothing of importance in the determination of Church doctrine, but the Third Council of Constantinople (680–1) ruled out a doctrine which, if accepted, would have taken the reality out of the human nature of Jesus—the doctrine that he had no human will distinguishable from the Divine Will, called the Monothelite (" One-will ") heresy. This heresy implied that there could have been no such thing in Jesus as the surrender of his human will to the Father, and made meaningless the conflict in his spirit, when he said, " Not my will, but Thine, be done."

The last and seventh of the Councils, recognized by Catholic and Orthodox alike as Œcumenical, the Second Council of Nicæa (787) decided a question which did not affect so vitally the Christian view of the nature of Jesus Christ, though the controversy had some connexion with it. It was the controversy which raged in the Eastern Empire between Iconoclasts (" Image-breakers ") and the majority of Christians in the eighth century. Was it right to make painted or sculptured representations of Jesus and the saints, and direct homage to such pictures or images? It affected the question of the nature of Jesus in so far as the defenders of image-worship argued that if Jesus was really a man, it was logical to hold that he could be represented in visible form. When the Jews had been forbidden to make images of God, the reason given (Deuteronomy iv. 12) had been that they had "seen no similitude" of God. In Jesus, God *had* shown Himself in visible form, and therefore if you asserted now that to make images was wrong, you in effect denied the Incarnation. We can see that the argument confused two different propositions—one, that Jesus had a body which was visible to people when he was on earth, the other that it was spiritually profitable for people to direct their devotions to a picture drawn according to the fancy of someone who had no means of knowing what Jesus had looked like. The second proposition may, or may not, be true, but it obviously does not follow logically from the first.

But in the course of argument about the relation of the Father and the Son another problem had come up. In the old baptismal formula, given by the Gospel of St. Matthew (xxviii. 19), the Spirit was named together with the Father and the Son. From the earliest times Christians had spoken continually about the Holy Spirit, but many Christians regarded the Spirit either as simply a mode of God's action, or as a kind of angel, a subordinate agent of God. Their view of God was binitarian, not trinitarian. About the beginning of the third century indeed the term *Trias* in Greek, *Trinitas* in Latin, came into use as denoting the Three mentioned together in the old formula, but the term did not necessarily imply belief in the Spirit as a "Person" co-equal with Father and Son. It was desirable that on this point too confusion of views should be brought to an end, and a doctrine laid down for which the Church as a whole would stand. This need was met by the First Council of Constantinople (381), the same council which condemned Apollinarianism. The Holy Spirit was affirmed to be a "Person (*Hypostasis*)" equal with the Father and the Son, "proceeding from" the Father. From now onward the term "Holy Trinity (*Hagia Trias*)" had the meaning which it keeps to-day, as an element of Catholic belief.

How far away it all seems from the vivid poetical words in which the Sermon on the Mount drove home upon men a tremendous ideal of conduct! What a pity, many people say around us, that men should not just have rested in the simple declaration of "values" by Jesus, instead of plunging into these abstruse metaphysical arguments, which were without spiritual profit, and were largely carried on by the use of ancient philosophical notions, grown meaningless in the light of modern thought. Perhaps no candid person can read the literature of those controversies without admitting repellent things about it. One is the universal assumption that anyone who holds a mistaken view on a difficult theological question can do so only by devilish malignity, so that vituperative rhetoric may with justice be poured upon an opponent. Well might anybody who knew of Christianity only some parts of its ancient controversial literature become anti-Christian! Its unpleasant characteristics are partly due to the Greek environment in which early Christianity arose; for with the Greeks interest in intellectual theory and its logical expression had been developed in a disproportionate way, and the whole education of the Græco-Roman world had become vitiated with rhetoric. Ancient Greek Stoics and Epicureans had fought passionately in public about their rival philosophies. There is thus some justification for people to-day thinking much in the old controversies deplorable. But to suppose that the Christians could have lived their life without any controversy at all shows an inability or an unwillingness to think. If Christians were going to come to the world with any affirmations about God, it was just intellectual sincerity for them to make up their minds what the words which they used meant. To-day, while the duty of being kindly and good-natured all round is very generally recognized, people often hardly regard it as a duty at all to think what their affirmations mean or what relation they bear to the facts of the Universe. If the essential thing about the Christian message was a new announcement of what God was, of what God had done and would do, the announcement could hardly be effective so long as Christians themselves had quite confused ideas of what the words which they used implied. They had somehow to explain what they meant when they made the two apparently contradictory assertions—that God was One, and that Jesus was, for worship and devotion, equivalent to God. It was certainly desirable that the Church as a whole should come to an agreement what explanation Christians really stood for. And it was impossible that such an agreement should be arrived at without discussion—without controversy, in which a man holding that one view was right tried to show that another view was wrong. It does not necessarily imply any want of Christian charity, if a man attacks with the utmost vigour a view which he believes to be wrong. What does imply a want of charity is if a man makes the honest holding of a view which he thinks mistaken to be a mark of moral turpitude in the other man, and attacks, not the view, but him. And such a want of charity was lamentably common in the old Christian controversialists. They had, no doubt, to safeguard the true meaning of the great Announcement, but even where they were right in seeing that this or the other affirmation, if followed out to its logical implications, would stultify something essential in the Announcement, they failed to recognize how largely men do not draw the logical conclusions from their beliefs—often very fortunately, since thus it is possible for men to be much better than their creed. The early Christian controversialist never seems to have said to himself, " Perhaps the man whom I am attacking is in God's sight a better man than I, because, although he is certainly wrong in this particular matter, he may turn the truth he does see to much finer account in practice than I do the truth which I see." But while a Christian's attitude to an individual person should be governed by the recognition that he may hold a poisonous doctrine and be a good man, that is something quite different from saying that a community ought to tolerate in its accredited teachers teaching which is logically incompatible with the belief for which the community stands. No one could reasonably charge the authorities of the early Church with fanaticism or intolerance because they deprived heretical teachers of their office. Even now this is often not seen by ordinarily intelligent people. When, for instance, the authorities of the Church of England recently deprived of his office a priest who began to teach Spiritualism, the cry of "persecution" was raised by certain people on the wholly irrelevant ground that the priest in question was a very good man. Many Buddhists and Mohammedans are exceedingly good men, but that would be no reason for the Church authorities allowing Buddhism or Mohammedanism to be taught from the pulpit. A Rationalist society which employed paid teachers to lecture against Christianity would not act unreasonably if it dismissed a lecturer who became converted and began preaching Christianity as an agent of the Society: it would be inept to urge against their action that the man dismissed had a beautiful character. While, then, controversy in the early Church was disfigured by the presupposition that anyone teaching error must necessarily be in a state of damnation, it was impossible, even had Christians shown the maximum of charity, that an agreement as to the meaning of the Gospel should be reached without a great deal of argument and controversy, and without the authorization of the community being withdrawn from a certain number of teachers.

But there is another ugly thing in the story of these controversies, the worldly force brought in to give prevalence to this or the other side. In 316 Constantine began it, by sending the North-African bishops who followed a certain Donatus into banishment and taking away their churches. After that the interference of the secular Power in the disputes of the Church was frequent. When Arius and the bishops who agreed with him refused to accept the decision of Nicæa, Constantine interned them in Illyricum. Then in 335 Constantine, who had been swung round temporarily to the other side, banished Athanasius, now Bishop of Alexandria, to Trèves. And so on through the succeeding centuries.

It may seem that decisions on theological questions arrived at under such conditions have little worth. Yet Roman Catholics and Greek Orthodox alike hold that the decisions of the seven Œcumenical Councils were infallible, and Anglo-Catholics believe this of the first six. Even the Protestant Reformed Churches, who do not believe in the necessary infallibility of Œcumenical Councils, have held, generally speaking, that the decisions reached at the First Council of Nicæa, the First Council of Constantinople, the Council of Chalcedon, and the Third Council of Constantinople were right, as against the views condemned. The Reformers still held fast to the Nicene and the "Athanasian" creeds. And it is probably over-hasty to regard the interference of the secular world as necessarily invalidating the decisions taken. For the great diffused force which in the last resort determined which way Councils decided moved to its end, impeded perhaps, but ultimately undiverted, by oscillations of Imperial policy. That force was the general sense of the Christian community, which by a kind of instinct rejected theories felt to be incompatible with its faith. The bishops who met in Council, some of them, no doubt, personally men of a poor enough sort, had behind them this volume of communal feeling, and their movements of mind and will were controlled by it, whether they were conscious of the control or not. If a Catholic holds that this general sense of the community, this instinct for choice and rejection, was itself controlled by the Spirit of the Lord in heaven, the historian cannot prove such a belief to be absurd.

But it may be said that beside the spirit shown in these controversies being deplorable, and beside the intrusion of worldly force and intrigue into their conduct, the dispute was essentially futile: it had to do with things so far outside the reach of the human mind, the precise metaphysical nature of Christ, the relation of "Persons" within the Godhead, that all argument about them between men is worse than ridiculous. This, of course, raises the question whether any affirmation at all can reasonably be made about the ground of the Universe. All one can say here is that God's being incomprehensible does not imply that no affirmation can reasonably be made about Him. The world we see is incomprehensible, in so far as its nature is still a problem for physicists and philosophers, yet certain affirmations can plainly be made about it ; human personality is still, as Tennyson called it, an abysmal depth, yet affirmations can be made about it. The early Christians, when they made affirmations about God, quite realized that God, in the totality of His being, is incomprehensible. Whether the particular affirmations they made are ones which a modern man can still reasonably make is, no doubt, a question. It does not lie within the scope of this little volume to offer a philosophical defence of Christian beliefs. But certain things anyone considering the history of Christianity, simply as human history, can see. One is that to make its affirmations the Christian Church sometimes used terms borrowed from the vocabulary of the Greek philosophical schools, terms belonging to ways of thought now obsolete. This implies that the old definitions cannot satisfy the intellectual inquiry of modern men ; if they are still used, it can only be because they are interpreted by other terms which have meaning for us. At the same time it may be wise for a Christian community at present to express its beliefs ceremonially in the old formula, because the community as a whole may agree that, as between the two views in conflict when the formula was framed, the truth was on the side of the view stated in the formula rather than on the other, and this measure of agreement implies a community of belief, up to a point, about the question which the formula tried in antiquated language to determine, whereas if a new formula had to be framed in modern language, all kinds of disagreement would come up which might split the community. The use of the old formula thus allows a larger freedom of thought without a rupture of unity, since its phraseology, recognized as humanly inadequate, ties down less than a modern formula would, subscription to which would be construed as implying an exact agreement with the verbal statements.[1]

Another thing which the historian can see is that whether the Christian belief about God was true or not, that belief, with all its consequences in devotion and in life, was bound up with the view of Jesus asserted at Nicæa. The key-word of the decision made at Nicæa, *homousios,* "of one substance," involves indeed the

[1] Something analogous may be seen in the sphere of art. A picture of heaven by Fra Angelico with archaic figures and a conventional gold background is more satisfying to us to contemplate than a modern picture of heaven which tried to be realistic would be. We are obviously not supposed to take the former picture as more than symbolical, whereas we should feel expected to believe, when we looked at a realistic picture, that heaven really was like that.

ancient Greek conception of *usia*, "substance," which it is very hard to fit to the universe as we see it to-day. And when we find that there were Christians who put forward an alternative term "*homoi-usios*," "of *similar* substance," and that the main body of the Church fought against this, the quarrel may seem lamentable hair-splitting. Some wit has made current an epigram that all this ado was about a single letter of the alphabet. That, however, although it sounds smart, is one of the most foolish would-be witticisms ever put forth, because the difference between two statements is not important according to the number of letters which distinguishes one from the other in writing. One might just as well say that the controversy between monotheists and polytheists, believers in God and believers in gods, was a dispute about a single letter! In regard to the Arian controversy, it is only a shallow view which can lead people to suppose that it was a fighting about metaphysical subtleties which had no bearing on devotion and life. The oneness of the Son with the Father, which the Greek term was chosen to express, made the whole difference to the Christian thought of God. This can be seen by an analogy. In the days of the War there were people who sneered when a father was spoken of as having "given a son." They implied that the real sacrifice was on the side of the son, not of the father. The sneer was cruel just to the extent to which each son was a part of the father's own life.

That differed from case to case, but it is true that no human persons can be so completely one that either can claim the whole sacrifice made by the other as his own. And if, when Christians said that God "so loved the world that He gave His only-begotten Son," they meant by God's Son a created Being not one with Himself, even though it were a Being "similar in substance" to God, then the Cross might show a good man, or an incarnate Angel, enduring pain by his own heroic choice, but it could no longer show God's love. God would simply have let someone else suffer, and that would be a cheap mode for God to show love. The very heart of the Christian faith was involved in the controversy between Arius and Athanasius.

It has to be grasped that the assertions about God embodied in the Christian doctrine of the Trinity, definitively formulated at Constantinople in 381, were not put forward as speculations men got out of their own heads. They purported to systematize a number of different statements found in the books of the New Testament, regarded not as statements which man of his own intelligence hazarded about God, but as statements which God Himself had put into the minds of men, consequently infallible. To-day many people would, no doubt, say that the statements in the New Testament books were not in that sense inspired, and cannot be combined in a single system, because they express different and incompatible ideas current in the Christian community when the New Testament books were written. In any case, an historian must pronounce that on the premisses of the Fathers assembled at Constantinople the statement of the doctrine of the Trinity and of the two natures of Christ logically followed. It was the only view which, taking all the statements of the New Testament as precisely true, framed them in a single formula. No doubt, to some extent, the several statements were not reconciled but simply put side by side, so that the formula, for instance, of the two natures of Christ does not offer an explanation, but presents a mystery. Yet it may have been vital that the belief in Christ's deity and the belief in Christ's real humanity should both have been held fast, whether any metaphysical formula reconciling the two beliefs finally satisfactory to the mind of man can ever be found or not.

In the fifth century the Latin-speaking churches of the West were agitated by a controversy of a different kind, a controversy which concerned, not the nature of God or of Christ, but the relation of the Divine Will and the human will in the work of salvation. The Church as a whole, indeed, pronounced on the controversy at the Council of Ephesus in 431; but Greek-speaking Christians were not generally interested in it, or even aware of its significance. It is called the Pelagian controversy from the British monk, Pelagius, whose teaching started it. Christians had always laid stress on the reality of Free Will in men, but had also laid stress on men being saved by Divine Grace, and the difficulty of reconciling the two had never been realized till an attempt was made to simplify the problem by making the human will practically everything, and reducing the action of Divine Grace to man's being presented with an ideal from outside—though Pelagius sought to save religion by insisting that, after all, man was created by God, his power of will was given him by God. The man who led the opposition to Pelagianism was one of the greatest figures in Christian history, indeed a man who was epoch-making in European culture and literature, the North-African Bishop of Hippo, Augustinus (354–430). He had been in his youth a semi-pagan, a teacher of Latin literature and rhetoric; then he had followed the Manichæan religion, a form of Gnosticism founded by a Babylonian called Mani in the middle of the third century, which had a great vogue for some centuries in the Nearer East; finally he had become a Christian. The account of his spiritual history up to his conversion, which he wrote in his *Confessions*, is one of the world's classics: no book of such a *genre* had ever been written before. As a Christian, he became a great teacher of the Western Church; his writings occupy many large volumes, and it is probably true that no other one man did so much to shape Christian thought in Europe up to the end of the Middle Ages. He was a man of intense religion and a powerful original thinker, with a bent to mystical exaltation which is often impressive and beautiful; at the same time, where his theology led him to terrible conclusions, his hard logic so eliminated natural human feeling that his personality strikes a chill, as contact might with a being from another planet. The doctrine that man could save himself by rightly directing his own will Augustine saw to be incompatible with the Christian attitude. The individual man did not start, as Pelagius supposed, with a nature which was a blank sheet, neither good nor evil, but with a nature already profoundly vitiated. Man had by heredity too sick a soul for it to be thinkable that he should by his own unaided choice direct his will aright. If he was to be saved, it could only be by Divine Grace entering into him mightily and turning his diseased will to good. Pelagius held the common-sense moral view which made it seem simple enough that man, with free will, should choose good in preference to evil: inherited sin was impossible, because sin could be nothing but a man's own wrong choice, and a man was under no compulsion to choose wrong. If there is anything at all in religion, the Pelagian view, for all its apparent reasonableness, excluded a perception of the deeper reality, and because Augustine was essentially religious, he felt the self-sufficient moralism of Pelagius to be profoundly wrong. Yet the problem of reconciling philosophically the operation of Divine Grace with the liberty of the human will Augustine, at the end of all his arguments, left an unsolved problem, and an unsolved problem it remains for Christians to-day. Nearly all the difficulties in the religious view of the world, when pushed home, turn out to be variations of this one great fundamental difficulty—the problem of evil, the problem of prayer, no less than the problem of salvation. Thus the controversy between Augustine and the Pelagians was only one form of a controversy which goes on in all theistic religions—not in Christianity alone[1]—and in one form or another is likely to go on indefinitely. And if it be made a reproach against Christians —or against Theists generally—that they create the difficulty for themselves by the arbitrary hypothesis of a God, they may reply that, even apart from any such hypothesis, the problem of the human will is there: it is just as hard to reconcile human choice, as we know it from within and regard it in practice, with scientific determinism.

While, however, the great body of Christian opinion ever since—not Catholic opinion only— has held that Augustine was, in his general attitude, right as against the Pelagians, the controversy in those days was mixed up with a number of beliefs which have no actuality for most educated men to-day, and some of which even modern Catholics, though those beliefs were firmly held by Augustine, recognize to be appalling. Augustine pictured man's

[1] For instance in the Bhakti form of Hinduism: see R. Otto, *India's Religion of Grace and Christianity*, 1930, pages 51–58.

supposed state of sinlessness before Adam's fall in a way which no one could entertain to-day: his belief that in consequence of a single act of disobedience committed by the first man all men inherit, not only a vitiated nature, but "original sin" in the sense that God can justly punish them for that alone by eternal torment, apart from any acts of sin they may individually commit, seems to us to-day only a horrible oddity in outworn human imaginations. The question of baptism also came largely into the controversy, inasmuch as Christians believed that by baptism a new supernatural life was introduced into man, which by God's continuous work of Grace could dominate the vitiated nature inherited from Adam and set men free from the burden of original guilt. In this connexion Augustine's view clashed with the Pelagian view regarding the reason why infants should be baptized. The Pelagians, contending that a man could not be guilty except for sins he had himself committed, asserted that unbaptized infants, dying before they could commit sin, entered into "eternal life," though they held that baptism conferred a higher privilege which unbaptized infants missed, that of entering into the "Kingdom of God." Augustine, maintaining that infants inherited from Adam the original guilt which was a sufficient ground for their damnation, apart from any actions of their own, asserted that all babies dying unbaptized would burn for ever in Hell, although he expressed a pious opinion that in their case the pain would not be so acute as in the case of actual sinners. He affirmed, as something obvious, that an enormously larger proportion of the human race would be damned than would be saved. He convicted the Pelagians, not ineffectively, of weak logic in making the distinction they did between entering into Life and entering into the Kingdom of God. And if he was charged with making God cruel in his doctrine of the eternal punishment of infants, his reply in substance was, "No, it is you who make God cruel, because the fact that infants suffer is an undeniable fact of the world, which you have only to look round to see. God *would* be cruel if He let guiltless beings suffer. If God is kind and just, no suffering without guilt. Since infants do suffer, they must in some way be guilty. Since they have no guilt of their own, they must inherit the guilt of Adam, in whom the whole human race sinned. If they inherit the guilt of Adam, and suffer for it to the extent we see, it is reasonable to believe that they suffer the rest of the penalty as well, eternal damnation." So did logic lead Augustine to his appalling conclusion; at the same time one must admit in it a kind of heroic determination to face the facts of the Universe even when they are terrible. For it is true that the suffering of infants is there, as a fact of the world, and that views like the Pelagian, which make everything straightforward and plain and morally trim, do not go deep enough.

But while those elements in Augustine's

doctrine are discarded, it is held by practically all Christians that he was right when he maintained that for every good movement of his will man had to thank the Grace of God. After Pelagianism had been condemned by the Church, some Christian teachers in the West put forward a doctrine, called " Semi-Pelagian," which sought to keep for man's unaided free will at any rate the first movement by which he gave himself to God: after that, they admitted, man owed all right movements of his will to God working in him, but it depended on the man alone in the first instance to decide whether he would or would not be receptive of God's Grace. Even this compromise Christian feeling repudiated: when a man looked back upon his spiritual history he must see no good in himself at all, from the very first stirring of his will towards God, which was not due to God's working in him, to God's sovereign unmerited Grace.

CHAPTER VI

THE CHRISTIAN EMPIRE

THE extraordinary change by which Christianity, instead of being the religion of a persecuted minority, became the religion of the Imperial court, made a great difference to the character of the Christian community. Christianity did not immediately become the official religion of the Roman Empire. Constantine continued during his lifetime to be formally *Pontifex Maximus* of the old religion of the Roman State, and he did not actually receive baptism till on his death-bed. For a time Christianity and Paganism existed side by side, tolerated equally. With the Emperor Gratian (375–83) the State began to take steps for the suppression of the old religion. Gratian refused to be *Pontifex Maximus*; the subsidy which the State had continued to make to various traditional forms of pagan worship was discontinued; the revenues of many temples and priesthoods were confiscated; the golden image of Victory in the Senate-house in Rome was removed. Theodosius I (appointed by Gratian Emperor for the Eastern half of the Empire 379, Sole Emperor 383–95) went further. He destroyed a number of temples, amongst them one of the most august of the old world, the temple of Sarapis at Alexandria. Then practices of the old religion were made legally punishable by a fine. Arcadius (395–408) and Honorius (395–423), the sons of Theodosius, confiscated all the revenues which yet remained to any temples. Justinian (517–65) made it impossible for pagans legally to own property, and he shut down the Academy (529), the School of Philosophy at Athens founded by Plato which had had a continuous existence of 900 years.

The Christian emperors thus quickly, with the approval of the Church, departed from the principle of toleration, which allows every subject of the State to follow any form of religion he chooses without incurring a legal penalty, so long as its practices do not conflict with the moral principles safeguarded by ordinary legislation. The method by which the Christian Empire suppressed the old religion was definitely persecution, even if persecution of a much milder kind than that which the pagan Empire had used against the Christians. Persecution in this case was successful. Many men who loved the great tradition of the Greek world had a sentimental attachment to the old religion; the word "Hellenes" was commonly used in those days to denote pagans in distinction from Christians. It was probably someone of such a temper who composed what was said to have been the last oracle delivered at Delphi to the emissaries of the Emperor Julian (331–63),

"Tell ye the King: It is fallen, the dwelling of wondrous adornment;
Gone are the booths of Apollo, the green oracular laurel;
Dumb the streams; dry, dry is the speech-giving water for ever."

But Paganism could not show any great roll of martyrs. Persecution was successful because the old system was really dead within, and the external force applied brought it altogether to the ground.

The new position which Christianity had acquired in the world made a greater difference to the character of Christianity than it did to the character of the world. If any Christian of the first century could have been brought to describe what, in his imagination, the world would become, supposing by some fantastic change the little congregation of Brethren obtained the supreme direction of the Roman Empire, it would certainly have been a very different world from the one he saw around him. The disappointing thing is that when the change came about, the world went on very much as before—the institutions of the State were the same, the behaviour of men in business and pleasure, slavery, wars. Almost immediately after having undergone persecution itself, the Church began to instigate the rulers of the world to persecute on its behalf. It was not only against Paganism that Christian rulers used the arm of the State, it was against forms of Christianity which the predominant Church regarded as heretical. The use of force to suppress divergent opinion has marked the history of Christianity down to modern times. Here again the great figure of St. Augustine appears on the threshold of Medieval Christianity in a sinister light. His authority more than any helped to establish persecution as a principle: he found sanction for it in the words of Jesus, "*Compel* them to come in" (Luke xiv. 23). Yet the Church's use of persecution cannot be fairly judged by those who suppose that it is a matter of indifference what people believe. It is really essential to the Christian view that false belief is a deadly evil. In regard to the killing of heretics, we find an acute thinker who looked at Christianity from a detached standpoint writing,

> "At any rate, the ostensible object of such horrors was Christian, and the indignation which professedly prompts them is also Christian, and the assumption they involve, that agonies of pain and blood shed in rivers are less evils than the soul spotted and bewildered with sin, is most Christian." [1]

Only it is possible to hold that false belief is a deadly evil, and yet hold that it is never right to compel anyone by the infliction of pains to profess to believe something which he does not believe, and seldom right to prevent anyone from freely putting before others a belief which he does hold.[2]

[1] Seeley, *Ecce Homo*, Chapter XXI (conclusion).

[2] The question of constraint used in the latter way is not so simple as the other. The laws of all civilized countries to-day limit liberty in the matter of expressing views on morals, and prohibit some kinds of action

To justify the forcible suppression of heretics, the Church often appealed to the laws of old Israel which commanded that anyone introducing idolatry or witchcraft into the community of Jehovah should be put to death. Hence some have represented the use of persecution in the Church as an evil inheritance from Judaism. But this mistakes the real character of Christian persecution. It is not derived either from the Hebraic or from the Hellenic antecedents of Christianity, taken separately, but is a curious combination of something got from the Jews with something got from the Greeks. The laws of old Israel surrounded with a horror of impiety practices such as idolatry which were an apostasy from the One God in action. But these abominations, for which the penalty was death, were always actions, or incitements to action, never the expression of opinions. It was the Greeks, as we have seen, for whom intellectual differences had such importance. It is true that, although the old Greek philosophers had contended about different views of the universe with intense polemic passion, the expression of opinion in the ancient Greek States was on the whole free. The idea, however, of suppressing wrong opinion

---

which are calculated to stimulate men to vice. No one, for instance, would be allowed by existing English Law to put forward freely in public a view of the world, however sincerely held, which commended homosexual relations. Catholics can, no doubt, argue that the force invoked by the Church for the suppression of poisonous opinions was only an extension of the same principle.

by force, which never occurs amongst the ancient Jews, does occur amongst the Greeks. Plato, in that picture of the ideal city-state, which he constructed in his old age, makes anyone professing atheism liable to imprisonment for five years, and, on a second conviction, to death.[1] Here, nearly 300 years before the appearance of Christianity, the principle of religious persecution for opinion was clearly laid down by the greatest of the ancient Greek philosophers. Christianity took from the Old Testament the particular tone of religious detestation which coloured its feeling towards heretics and its sanction for putting them to death in dreadful ways: but it took from the Greeks its idea of what constituted punishable impiety, wrong opinion.

One consequence of Christianity's becoming the professed religion of the Empire, was an accentuation of the difference between clergy and laity. In the early days the bishops and presbyters who presided in the communal acts of worship were in ordinary life indistinguishable from other members of the community, and they usually supported themselves by some secular employment. After the Empire had become Christian, the Christian priests began to be given a position of special privilege in the State. Pagan priests in old days had been immune from a number of burdens borne by ordinary men, in regard to taxes, and so on: similar privileges were now conferred upon Christian

[1] *Laws*, 909 *c*.

priests. Then regular salaries were assigned them from a fund which grew by the confiscation of the property of pagan temples and fresh donations. The bishops were given by the State a disciplinary power in certain respects even over laymen, and a power of protecting within certain limits persons liable to punishment by the State tribunals. The Church inherited sanctuary-rights from the temples. Thus the clergy became not only an order in the Church, but an influential class in the State. It was not for a long time that the clergy came to be distinguished by a special dress. As late as 428 the Bishop of Rome rebuked the bishops of Gaul because they wore a garb different from that of ordinary men. The differentiation of the clerical dress was a consequence of the gradual conquest of the Empire by northern barbarians. Varieties of the barbarian garb, short tunic and trousers, with long hair, came to be the dress of ordinary men. It was thought decent that the clergy should retain the long robe of the Roman Empire, and cut their hair short, as Romans had done. After the sixth century this traditional Roman dress, which marked them out from other men, was made obligatory for the clergy by ecclesiastical authority.

The administrative organization of the Church in the Christian Empire had necessarily become much more elaborate. The bishop of the capital city of a province of the Empire came to have an authority over the other bishops of the province, and to be styled the "Metropolitan."

Then the bishops of five cities—Rome, Constantinople, Alexandria, Antioch and Jerusalem—came to bear the title of "Patriarch" (used officially in the ninth century), which indicated their authority as one superior even to that of Metropolitans. Finally the Western Patriarchs, the bishops of Rome, obtained general recognition throughout the West of their claim to have authority, as Vicars of Christ, over the whole Church upon earth. Curiously enough, the title which came to be popularly attached to the Bishop of Rome in this capacity was taken from the nursery, *papa*, "daddy." It is applied as a term of ridicule by Tertullian to Callistus (Bishop of Rome 219–223), whose pretensions he thought excessive. In the fourth century it was often used seriously as a honorific form of address in writing to bishops. The first-known instance in which it is used as a distinctive title of the Bishop of Rome occurs in the writings of Ennodius of Pavia, early in the sixth century. In English the title has become "Pope."

Whether such authority did, or did not, belong to the Bishop of Rome by right in the first centuries, it was possible for so good a churchman as St. Cyprian, Bishop of Carthage in the third century, still to be ignorant of it, for the doctrine which he championed was that all bishops equally embodied the one episcopal authority, and he opposed on that ground the claims put forward by the Bishop of Rome. Roman Catholics, who maintain that all the authority belonging to the Pope according to the Vatican decree of 1870 belonged just as much by right to the first Bishops of Rome, admit that it took some centuries for the supremacy of the Pope to be generally recognized by Latin-speaking Christianity. They admit that the supremacy, as it was later understood, cannot be conclusively demonstrated from the utterances of Christian writers in the first centuries. Modern Protestant scholars, on the other hand, admit that from the end of the first century, a peculiar prestige attached to the Christian community in Rome and its official head, partly from the connexion of the church in Rome with St. Peter and St. Paul, partly from the fact that Rome was the chief city of the Empire, partly from the prominent part taken by Roman Christians in works of Christian beneficence. The Bishop of Rome is shown by the documents paternally solicitous for the affairs of other Christian churches, and intervening from time to time with a weight of authority. Writing of the fourth century, Harnack, a Liberal Protestant, says, "Even in the eyes of Eastern Christians the Bishop of Rome had something special attaching to him, which no other bishop had, a halo which gave him a quite peculiar authority."[1] There is this measure of agreement to-day between Roman Catholic and Protestant scholars regarding the historical data. The disagreement is in regard to the background which must be reconstructed by his-

[1] *Dogmengeschichte* (4th Edn., Vol. II, p. 103).

torical imagination or by faith behind the data. Here the controversy turns on the passage in the first Gospel (Matthew xvi. 17–19), in which Jesus is represented as calling St. Peter "the Rock" upon which he will build his church, and as giving him "the keys of the Kingdom of heaven." The first instance known of the reference of this text to the claims of the Bishop of Rome is by Tertullian, who supposes that Callistus might appeal to it to support his (as Tertullian regarded them) unwarrantable pretensions. It came afterwards to be the chief scriptural foundation for the Pope's claims. Old-fashioned Protestants refuted the Roman argument by denying that the text implied the conferring upon Simon Peter of any position of unique authority in the community, by denying also that Peter was called the Rock; the word for "rock" in Greek, they insisted, was feminine, *petra*, while Peter's name was masculine. Modern Protestant scholars recognize that this old Protestant argument was worthless: the passage undoubtedly does imply a position of peculiar authority given to St. Peter, and in the Aramaic which Jesus spoke the name given to Simon, *Kephā*, does not differ in form from the word for "rock." Modern Protestants of the critical school would mostly hold that the passage was not an authentic utterance of Jesus, but was imported into the first Gospel because this emanated from some circle which desired to magnify the authority of Peter in the primitive community. But even if the saying was really uttered by Jesus, Protestants would contend, it contains nothing to show that the authority conferred personally upon Peter was to be transmitted to the Bishops of Rome. This is a gap which Roman Catholics fill by faith in the teaching of the Church as it came to be authoritatively defined.

In the Christian Empire the Church thus formed a kind of spiritual State alongside of the earthly State: it had its own separate organization, its own hierarchy of office-bearers, its own large property, its own philanthropic institutions, orphanages, schools, hospitals, its own disciplinary tribunals. Only it had no material force at its disposal, no army and no police. If force was required for the suppression of heresy, or for any other purpose, the Church could appeal only to the State to lend its arm. And this the Christian State was in most cases willing to do. No heretic was ever put to death by the Church: the Church handed heretics over to the authorities of the State on the understanding that the State would put them to death.

With the influence which the Church had upon the State after Constantine, it may seem strange that it did so little to reform the institutions of the world. Even in the sphere of Law, punishments in the Christian Empire were, generally speaking, more drastic than they had been in the old Roman Empire. Slavery went on as a legal institution: the property owned by the Church included a large number of slaves. It was probably inevitable that wars between the Roman Empire and non-Christian peoples, Germans and Persians, should go on under Constantine. Perhaps the first time when Christians met Christians, to kill each other in battle, apart from the suppression of rebellions within the Empire, was at Pollentia, on April 6, 402, when the Christian Goths who had followed the standards of Alaric in his invasion of Italy, were attacked by the Imperial general Stilicho, whilst they were celebrating Easter. During the centuries which followed wars between Christians were to be as common as wars in the old pagan world.

Of course, the truth is that the world was very far from being converted to Christianity. Vast masses of people everywhere now called themselves Christians and were formally incorporated in the Christian Church, who were as pagan as ever in heart. This made a great difference to Christianity. It has not yet, in the sixteen centuries since, recovered from the influx of worldly elements which began under Constantine. In addition to this, the ancient Græco-Roman society, when the Emperors embraced Christianity, was breaking up. The State had become a bureaucracy ; the inhabitants of the Empire were impoverished and ground down by taxation ; the forces of the State were composed of northern barbarians. Peoples who have their fighting done for them by others inevitably fall into subjection to those others. Barbarian chieftains, who were given the position of Imperial generals, came more and more to dominate the government, whilst barbarians settled in numbers upon the Mediterranean lands. From the latter part of the fifth century the titular Roman Emperor with his seat at Constantinople had only precarious and intermittent control over the Latin-speaking lands—Italy and the West, till finally in the ninth century a German chieftain, Charles the Great (Charlemagne) set himself up in the West as a rival and founded the new "Holy Roman Empire," whose Emperors were Germans. Europe had entered the "Dark Ages."

In such a time of decay, disruption and unsettlement, the Church would have had little chance, even if it had desired, to recast the institutions of the world. Beside that, the institutions, belonging to a great civilization hundreds of years old, seemed an essential part of the earthly order of things. In truth, to change them radically never seems to have occurred to the Church as a thing that it should try to do. The main reason for this was that the Church regarded it as its mission to fit men for the eternal Divine society beyond the earthly order of things, and it would not have seemed worth while to try to make the world essentially different from what it was. Under the old pagan Emperors, the attitude of Christians to the State had been partly one of repudiation, in so far as the State, impelled by Satan, demanded of them things which conflicted with a Christian's duty to God, partly one of obedience, in so far as the powers that be were ordained of God to keep public order. But even when the State ceased to be pagan, its institutions were still for Christians those of a world soon to pass away. Slavery, war, trade, forcible punishment, were all things incompatible with the ideal, but the ideal had ceased to be possible when man fell, and for fallen man the rule of force in the State was necessary, partly as a judgment of God upon sin, partly as a restraint upon fallen man's violent propensities. The return of Christ upon the clouds, which the first Christians had expected at any moment, had, it is true, been relegated to a future rather further off, but not, it was still believed, very far off, and in any case the imagination of heaven and hell, one or other of which certainly awaited every individual in a few years, vividly possessed the minds of Christians. And it should be recognized that any religion which believes in an eternal destiny for man beyond death, and has the courage of its convictions, must properly be "other-worldly" in laying its main stress upon preparation for the world beyond. It is perfectly logical for people who do not believe in any life beyond this to regard the improvement of conditions in this world as the only thing that matters, but to profess belief in an eternal world and not recognize it as supremely important is patently absurd.

While, however, the Church did not try to change the institutions of the world, it did concern itself with mitigating their consequences in detail, where these consequences produced sin or suffering, and with so changing the inner attitude of men that some things, evil in themselves, would cease to matter. In those days, when the economic decay produced widespread misery, the Church carried on a vast work of relief. The great possessions, in money, in kind and in land, bestowed upon the Church in the centuries following Constantine, were held professedly in trust for the poor, and were in fact largely used for succouring the poor. Hostels for the reception of indigent strangers were erected by the Church in a great many towns, and their name in Latin (*hospitalia*) passed to the houses for tendance of the sick, which the Church was the first to erect in Europe, probably as early as the fourth century. Or again, men could cease to feel the burden of some things belonging to this world but incompatible with the ideal of human society—social inequalities, slavery—by entering in spirit even here into the heavenly world. Christian master and slave did not cease to be unequal in regard to the things of this world, but they were "equal before God"; and so far as they entered by common worship into the spiritual sphere, there was no inequality any more. This was not merely a matter of theory: no doubt in innumerable cases the actual relations between Christian master and slave were in daily practice transformed by it. The very inequality might be used on either side as a means of spiritual training, willed for each by God in this transitional state. It was held up as, in most cases, a good work if a Christian master set his slaves free, though the Church retained apparently the slaves who were Church property without feeling that it did them any wrong.

The leaders of the Church, from the position of dignity accorded them by the State, and their control of the Church property, had an influence which they used on occasion even against the Imperial Power for the protection of the weak. When Theodosius I perpetrated a massacre at Thessalonica (he had some ground for extreme indignation against the people of the city who had begun committing atrocities in a discreditable quarrel with the Imperial authorities) the great Bishop of Milan, St. Ambrose, repelled the Emperor from communion till he had done public penance (390). A pagan historian of the latter part of the fourth century describes the worldly state and sumptuous living of some of the prince-bishops of the time, though he speaks at the same time of bishops of the provincial towns whom he knew as men of self-denying life, dressed in a garb like that of the poor.[1]

Even before Constantine, with accommodation to the world, life in the Christian community had sometimes sunk to a level much lower than that of the first days, but after masses of men had become Christians in name, there was hardly a possibility of keeping up the intense religious life which had been possible within small societies surrounded by an alien world. Jesus had set before his disciples a heroic demand, self-

[1] *Ammianus Marcellinus* XXVII, 3, 15.

devotion and self-sacrifice for the cause going to the extreme length, and in the early Church such heroism was often called for. The possibility of martyrdom always there, and those who actually underwent martyrdom, or by enduring torture became "confessors," kept alive in the mind of the community the heroic element in the faith. After Constantine, the days of martyrdom seemed over in the Roman Empire, and yet a picture of the Christian life which made it merely a well-conducted routine, at peace with society, could not satisfy all Christians. There was something in the human spirit which craved the exaltation of great self-sacrifice and great hardships faced and conquered; some substitute was wanted for martyrdom. Had the Church conceived a scheme for remodelling the institutions of the world nearer to the Christian ideal, it may be that in such an enterprise satisfaction would have been offered to the more ardent Christian spirits. But such an enterprise, as we have seen, never occurred to the Church. Satisfaction was found in another direction, not in changing the institutions of the world, but in creating little social islands, within which a life corresponding to the Christian ideal, as it was conceived, of communist brotherhood, manual labour, extreme renunciation and sexual continence, could be exhibited by those who aimed at perfection. The days which followed the conclusion of peace between the Church and the Empire, were the days which saw the spread of monasticism within the Church.

The distinctive mark of monasticism was the formation of ascetic societies, separate from the world, the members of which lived in obedience to a rule drawn up by the founder.[1] They began amongst the Christians of Egypt; someone who bore the Latin name of Antonius (St. Anthony, 260 to 360) organized his disciples as a community in the desert, though his personality is clouded with later legend, and the "Rule" ascribed to him is not authentic. In any case, communities of ascetics sprang up at this time in the deserts bordering the valley of the Nile, and from Egypt they spread rapidly to Palestine, Sinai, and Syria. The great Cappadocian Father, St. Basil of Cæsarea (about 330–79), laid down principles for the monastic communities of the Greek-speaking half of the Empire, and his name has ever since been associated with monasticism in the Greek Church. Before the end of the fourth century, monastic communities were to be found in numbers in Italy, Gaul and Spain. In the sixth century, the Italian St. Benedict (480–540) established monasteries, first at Subiaco and then at Monte Cassino, which rose to pre-eminent prestige, and the name of St. Benedict became for Latin

[1] Strictly speaking, it is a misnomer to describe such societies as "monastic" and their members as "monks," since the Greek word *monachoi* means "solitary ones," and was originally applied to hermits, in distinction from ascetics living in communities. But usage in all European languages has long given the term "monk" a meaning equivalent to the more correct, but now almost obsolete term, cenobite, the member of a community (*koinobios*).

Christendom what the name of St. Basil was for Greek.

Extreme forms of self-torture, such as those practised by Indian *sanyassis*, were not regarded as desirable in Christian monasticism, though some of the solitary ascetics in Eastern Christianity practised austerities not unlike the Indian ones—the "stylites" who never descended from the top of a column, the "dendrites" who never descended from a tree. But the great monastic rules excluded such excesses and combined religious exercises with useful manual labour—tilling the ground or weaving or building or copying manuscripts. The essential thing was that each monastery should be a society, in which every member renounced private property and the worldly interests which competed with religious devotion, and subordinated himself wholly to the community.

Asceticism is found all the world over in one form or another: but it has various motives and in consequence great differences of character. Amongst primitive peoples the temporary endurance of privation and pain is commonly part of the tribal rites by which boys are initiated into manhood, and may have originally been meant as a test of their endurance as fighters. In India the acquisition of magical powers is specially connected with self-torture. The sage Visvamitra, we are told, acquired such power in this way that the gods were terrified and did all they could to stop him. In Christian asceticism, though the power to work miracles has commonly been regarded as a proper consequence of great sanctity, its acquisition is never put forward as a motive for asceticism. Another motive for self-mortification has been the idea that some Divine Power is angry and may be pacified if the sinner inflicts punishment upon himself. In India, where the idea of sin as deserving punishment is faint, this motive is not prominent; but Christianity inherited from its Hebraic antecedents a strong sense of the guilt of sin and God's wrath against sin, and the idea that pain inflicted by a man upon himself might win his deliverance from the pain which would otherwise be inflicted upon him by the Divine judgment after death, was certainly one of those which operated widely in Christian asceticism. Yet fear of punishment would be regarded as a low motive by all the worthier representatives of Christianity, and asceticism actuated by such a motive implies a conception of God and of man's relation to Him which belongs rather to some of the pagan cults of the Hellenistic East than to Christianity.[1] One motive in Christian asceticism was quite peculiar to it—the desire to imitate Jesus. Here the motive was love, not fear. In some men the devotion and gratitude called out by the thought of the Divine self-sacrifice and love embodied in Jesus impelled them to a life of mortification and self-denial, the dedication of themselves wholly to God in response. But perhaps the most widely

[1] Steinleitner, *Die Beicht im Zusammenhange mit der sakralen Rechtspflege in der Antike* (1913).

operative motive was one which is also found urging men to asceticism outside Christianity—the sense of an inner competition between spiritual interests and other interests connected with worldly ambition or bodily pleasure, a competition which necessitates the cutting off of those other interests as completely as possible if the spiritual interests are to have room for free expansion. All the negative side of such asceticism—the suppressions, the mortifications—serve a great positive end: life on its lower levels is negated, in order that life of a higher kind may abound.

Of all interests competing with the soul's converse with God the sexual interest was the most obvious. Again, we have here nothing peculiar to Christianity: all religions have felt that there was something in the sexual interest, with its pervasive excitement, which had in various ways to be negated—usually by temporary abstinence—for the purposes of the cult; all ideas of winning deliverance for the higher life—whether amongst Indian sages or amongst Greek philosophers—have involved a man's obtaining mastery over sexual passion.[1] Fourth-century Christianity went so far as to consider sexual desire essentially evil and the life of complete abstinence the only life which could be Christian in the fullest sense. A considerable number of Christians regarded marriage as definitely wrong. Professor Burkitt

[1] E. Fehrle, *Die kultische Keuschheit im Altertum*, 1910.

thinks it probable that in the early Syriac-speaking Church no one was accepted for baptism unless he was prepared to abstain from all sexual relations.[1] But this view the Church as a whole condemned, and it appears in Church History as the "Encratite" heresy. Yet, even if marriage was pronounced an honourable estate, the life of complete abstinence was held to be higher.

This conception of sexual desire as essentially evil and unclean was not, as we have seen, something which Christianity brought into the Græco-Roman world, but something which infiltrated into Christianity from that world. From the sixth century B.C., when the Orphics spread through the Greek world with their motto "The body a tomb," there had been this ascetic strain in Greek society, opposed indeed to the temper of Greek society as a whole, stamping as hostile to the soul all emotions and cravings which had a strong bodily note. It came out markedly in Plato. But in the first centuries of the Christian era it had got immense extension in the Neo-pythagorean and Neo-platonist beliefs which ran through the Græco-Roman world. Gnosticism generally was characterized by the teaching that the body was evil. In the fourth century it was strongly represented in Manichæan religion, the crowning product of Gnosticism. It is hardly to be wondered at that Christianity, which had in it already an element of asceticism and regarded

[1] *Early Eastern Christianity*, p. 129.

sexual passion as something to be kept sternly under control, should have absorbed this idea, rife everywhere in its environment, that sexual desire was actually evil. What saved the Christian Church from going further than it did in that direction was its Jewish antecedents. Cleaving to the Old Testament against Gnostic depreciation, it was bound to the view that the material world was created good, and that even in the present abnormal state of the world a great deal of the original goodness remained side by side with the evil; it was further bound to the ideal of patriarchal family life which the Old Testament presented. It was of immense importance that one of its moral handbooks, regarded as Divinely inspired, was the book of *Ecclesiasticus*.[1] Christians might explain that under the conditions of the present age celibate life was preferable to married life, but with the Old Testament before them they could not regard married life as in itself evil.[2]

The active mind of St. Augustine found a way of reconciling the belief that sexual desire was

[1] One of the books of the old Christian Bible cut out of the Protestant Bible at the Reformation.

[2] It would not be true to say that in Rabbinical Judaism there is no trace of the idea that sexual desire is essentially evil. In that strange medley, out of which so many different doctrines, mutually contradictory, may be fished by those who go a-questing, there are sayings which identify the *evil* impulse in human nature (the *yetser ha-ra*) with the physical passion inseparable from even the legitimate procreation of children. See Strack and Billerbeck's *Kommentar zum Neu. Test.*, IV, pp. 468 ff.

essentially evil with the belief that conjugal life was a relative good. St. Augustine's doctrine is indeed more extreme than Catholic doctrine eventually was, in condemning all sexual desire. The Manichæans, to whom Augustine had belonged before his conversion, taught that it was an evil act to bring children into the world, and Augustine's opponents sometimes said that his condemnation of all sexual desire was un-Christian, a relic of Manichæism still clinging to him. Nothing made him more indignant. Not so, he taught that to generate children in the normal way of nature, in legitimate wedlock, was a good act; what was evil was the emotional excitement which accompanied the act. If his opponents said that this was an essential part of human nature, as created by God, and could not therefore be evil, St. Augustine said, No; it did not belong to human nature in its original state, as created by God; it was a consequence of the Fall. Had the Fall never occurred, man would have reproduced his kind precisely as he does now; only the act would have been one of calm and deliberate reason, as unemotional as the act by which I put out an arm to take a book down from a shelf. It was part of the degradation of man since the Fall that he could not now perform the act of generation without *libido*, which was wholly evil, not evil in excess only, but evil in any the least degree. All that a Christian could do now was either to abstain altogether from bringing the evil thing into play —the nobler choice—or, as a second best, utilize the evil thing for a good purpose, the procreation of children in legitimate Christian wedlock.

In quite early days every Christian had felt that Christianity made an immense demand upon him and he had had to be ready at any moment to forgo, for the sake of Christ and the Gospel, the things upon which the hearts of men were ordinarily set. But now that external conformity to Christianity had become so much easier, we see the aspiration, the bent to renunciation, which had once run through the whole Christian body, concentrate itself in smaller groups separated from the rest of the body. It is like the phenomenon of curdling, when instead of the milk having a uniform consistency right through, some of its constituents coagulate and leave the rest watery. Perhaps it was the only way, in the circumstances of the time, by which a Christian life of distinct quality could be saved, but the curdling has entailed a difficulty for Catholicism ever since—the difficulty of the double standard in the Christian life. It has since then seemed possible to be a Christian and deliberately choose a manner of life lower than the highest. Since the charge of recognizing such a double standard has been one of those most persistently urged by Protestants against Catholics in the last four centuries, it may be in place here to try to make the points at issue clearer. That in the Christian body there are differences of function is agreed on both sides. Nor can Protestants consistently deny that some functions are more honourable than others, or that, if the voluntary endurance of great pains and privations is required for the performance of certain functions, those who perform them stand higher than ordinary Christians in the Church's roll of honour. Missionaries, for instance, who have done their work at the cost of great sufferings and renunciations are habitually held up in Protestant religious literature as Christian "heroes." The charge really brought against Catholics is not that they recognize such a difference between higher and lower kinds of Christian service, but that they seem to make it optional for each individual whether he adopts the higher or the lower life. According to the Protestant theory, each individual has a particular work allotted to him by God, and to perform that faithfully is the highest thing which he can possibly do: it is wrong for anyone to aim at any standard lower than the highest possible for *him*. In a battle those detached for some operation which requires extraordinary endurance and courage perform a service in itself more glorious than that of those appointed to a post outside the danger-zone; yet the most meritorious work which those in the safe position can do is the work assigned them. The Catholic may reply that this view is precisely the one implied in his doctrine of "vocation": certain individuals only are "called" by God to the monastic life, and it would be wrong for anyone else to adopt it without such "vocation." Now if this idea of "vocation" were consistently carried through, the difference between the

Catholic and the Protestant view would perhaps disappear: then in Catholicism the individual would not be offered the option between a higher and a lower mode of life. Yet the Roman doctrine regarding works of "supererogation," that is good works which a man can do in excess of the strict requirements of duty, does seem to imply that there is an option for the individual whether he will aim at "perfection," or only at a lower grade of Christian virtue, and in regard to the figure of the soldiers in battle just adduced a Catholic might say that, as a matter of fact, for an enterprise of especial danger a general often does call for volunteers and detach those who offer themselves. In the same way God may call for volunteers for the hardest kind of Christian life. This may not logically be quite reconcilable with the doctrine of "vocation" (unless a man without a vocation can get a vocation by desiring it), though Protestants can hardly with reason repudiate the idea, so long as they themselves go on speaking of young men who adopt the missionary life as missionary "volunteers." Yet the Protestant theory maintains that it is impossible for a man to do more than his duty, and it is wrong for him to do less: his duty requires him to achieve the maximum of good within his power. The fact remains that in practice the specialization of certain renunciations, chiefly in the monastic life, has meant that ordinary Christians in Catholicism have often aimed at what they knew to be a lower standard, with the result that their lives have been little different from what they would have been, had they not been Christians at all. A Roman Catholic poet has described how, while the idea of the heroic life naturally attracts the young, he himself, as he grew older, found it appropriate to aim ever lower and lower in his spiritual aspiration.[1] The current Catholic usage which makes the term "religious" life mean a monastic life, even if justifiable with sufficient explanation, can hardly fail to have for the ordinary man a suggestion which Protestants may reasonably regard as unfortunate.

One may notice the confusions which arise, when comparisons are made between the Catholic and Protestant ideals of life, from the double standard in Catholicism not being taken into account. It is, for instance, common to hear the gloomy restrictions of Puritanism contrasted by Catholics with the free natural enjoyment allowed by Catholic religion. The truth, of course, is that most of the restrictions connected with Puritanism, and other renunciations besides, belong to Catholic life on the higher level, the monastic, and the Catholic life which, in contrast with Puritanism, appears so free in enjoyment is the lower life of the ordinary man. The restrictions in Protestant Puritanism are less severe than those in Catholic monasticism, but whereas the Catholic confines his restrictions to a relatively small band of specialists, the Puritan seeks to extend his to the whole Christian

[1] Coventry Patmore, *The Unknown Eros*, XXI, "Faint yet Pursuing."

community. The milk in its uncurdled state is thicker than the whey, but not so thick as the curds. When it is the curds in Catholicism which are compared by Protestants with the non-Catholic life then it is Catholicism which is represented (it may be misrepresented) as gloomy and inhuman; one may think of the well-known poem of Stevenson's, "Our Lady of the Snows."

From the fourth century till to-day monastic societies have been a characteristic of Catholic Christianity. They have often in practice fallen short of their ideal. Those who collect things to the discredit of Medieval Catholicism can find plenty of material in the documents for presenting monks and nuns in an odious or ridiculous light. Over and over again men of ardent spirit in the Church carried out a reformation of the monasteries and convents—a reformation which had obviously become a crying need. Yet the ideal was never wholly forgotten, and although some monks and nuns fell far short of it, there were others who exhibited a spiritual life of wonderful quality. Beside the cultivation of such an inner life, beside the specially religious effects which the monastic system was intended in the first instance to produce, a valuable contribution was made by the monks, in the West at any rate, through those centuries of disturbance and barbarism, to the temporal welfare of men. It was mainly through the monasteries that the Church carried out its extensive work of poor relief. The monks' agricultural labours "resulted in the clearing of a large part of the waste-land of Europe."[1] The schools in which all the learning that had survived from the wreck of the ancient civilization was passed on to future generations were mostly monastic. It was in the monasteries that books were preserved and copied. The missionaries who carried Christianity to the heathen barbarians of Northern or Central Europe were regularly monks. A Protestant historian writes:

"Though it is only within a small circle shut off from the rest of the world, yet here the ideas of work found in the New Testament may be seen realized. Work is performed because God has commanded it; each man does his allotted task perseveringly; work and prayer are combined; work alternates with rest, and the object of the work is not merely self-regarding; the worker seeks not to get something for himself, but to serve others."[2]

"Thus the monasteries," another German Protestant writes, "in their ascetic practice and in their existence as small shut-off societies, were the very guardians and radiating centres of all that could at that time be called Christian culture."[3]

---

[1] Hastings, *Enc. of Rel. and Eth.*, article "Monasticism," by Abbot Cabrol, p. 784.

[2] Von Schubert, quoted by E. Troeltsch in the passage referred to in the next note.

[3] E. Troeltsch, *Soziallehren*, p. 177.

CHAPTER VII

THE MIDDLE AGES

THE division of the Roman Empire into an Eastern half, whose dominant language was Greek, and a Western half, whose dominant language was Latin—a division which became fixed after Constantine—was of consequence for the Christian Church. Without any formal division of the Church immediately resulting, the mass of Latin-speaking Christians and the mass of Greek-speaking Christians developed separate interests and modes of thought and feeling. When the German invasions in the fifth century tore the Latin West altogether away from the authority of the Greek-speaking "Roman" Emperor, whose seat was Constantinople, the Western Church went its own independent way.

All the Christianity which was in future centuries to count as an important factor in the world, was developed from the Christianity of the Latin West. Eastern Christianity turned into a formal stereotyped tradition which sometimes appears in the modern world like a gilded mummy. In the fourth century Greek Christianity had in the Cappadocian Fathers—Basil,

Basil's brother, Gregory of Nyssa, and Gregory of Nazianzus—men who stood in the first rank among the writers and thinkers of their time and made an individual contribution to Christian thought. Somewhat later it had in St. John of Damascus (about 676–757) a theologian who presented a systematic and philosophic statement of the Christian faith, as understood in the Orthodox Church. But the process of Christian thought after this in the Greek East was arrested. The writings of St. Basil and St. John of Damascus continued to be read, but there was no further play of original thought upon the substance of the faith. In the Eastern (Byzantine) Empire the State was an unbroken continuation of the old Roman Empire, and the Church remained in such subordination to the Imperial court as had marked its position under Constantine and his immediate successors. It became a department of the State, whilst the Emperor on his side was invested with a sacred character. No Patriarch of Constantinople, though called "Œcumenical," could have the position of a Pope in the Christian West.

In some of the Eastern provinces of the Roman Empire the old native languages survived as the tongue of the common people under the predominance of Greek in the upper stratum, and when Christianity spread through the population as a whole, it brought into existence a Christian literature in these languages, Syriac in Mesopotamia, Armenian in Armenia, Coptic in Egypt, Ethiopic in Abyssinia. This Oriental

Christian literature was all either translated from Greek or took its ideas from the Greek Christian tradition; it brought nothing new of value to enrich Christian thought; its forms, however, showed some distinctively national characteristics, and with the new self-assertion of the old languages against Greek, there went a certain national self-assertion in ecclesiastical matters against the predominance of Constantinople. It was to some extent nationalist feeling which led the bulk of the Christians of Egypt in the fifth century to embrace the Monophysite heresy in opposition to the Orthodoxy of the Imperial court (a division which still to-day continues between the Egyptian Copts and the Greek Orthodox Church) and led a mass of the Syriac-speaking Christians to embrace Nestorianism.

The career of Nestorianism in the East beyond the bounds of the Roman Empire has been a remarkable one. As early at any rate as the sixth century they had established a Christian community in South India which still survives in the important body of "Syrian Christians" (about 300,000), though the greater part of the community has now attached itself to the Roman Church, and the remainder have deserted Nestorianism for its opposite, the Monophysite doctrine. In China the success of the Nestorian missions was still more astounding. In the eighth century several Emperors showed Christianity marked favour, and it almost looked as if China, like Europe, was to have its Constantine. Then political events turned against the Church and Chinese Nestorian Christianity withered away.

Yet in the thirteenth century there was still a Nestorian Christian Church amongst the Mongols in China. One monk whose home was at Pekin made a journey, of which an account in Syriac remains, to visit the Christians of the West, and had audience of Edward I at Bordeaux in 1287.[1]

Disagreements between Rome and the Greek bishops on questions of doctrine or jurisdiction go back to A.D. 500. In the latter part of the ninth century the disagreement became acute: at a Synod held at Constantinople in 867 the Greek Patriarch actually caused the Latin Pope to be pronounced anathema. At the Council of 879–80, however, also held at Constantinople (a Council not recognized by Rome), the Patriarch of Constantinople conceded the Pope a primacy in the West, but in the West only. In practice the two sections of the Church acquiesced after this in a division of territory, till Pope Leo IX (1049–54) brought about a renewal of the quarrel by asserting his authority over the Greek-speaking Christians of South Italy and Sicily. Then the rupture was definite and final. A Papal Bull placed in 1054 on the altar of St. Sophia in Constantinople excluded all who followed the Greek Patriarch from communion with Rome: the Greek Patriarch on his

[1] A. C. Moule, *Christians in China before* 1550. S.P.C.K., 1930, pp. 94 ff.

side excommunicated the Roman Church. The division between the Roman Church and the Greek Orthodox Church has continued till to-day. Though, however, Rome regards the Greek Orthodox Church as schismatic, in so far as it refuses obedience to the divinely appointed representative of Christ upon earth, Rome nevertheless recognizes the orders of the Orthodox Church as valid and holds that Christ is really present upon its altars. Rome will not do as much in the matter of Anglican orders.

It must be remembered that Greek and Eastern Christianity was, from the rise of Islam in the seventh century, subjected to a far more severe pressure from that new militant power than the Christianity of the West. In a way Islam might be counted rather as a Christian heresy than as an altogether alien religion. For while Mohammed got most of the material of the Koran direct from Judaism, he took over some noteworthy elements from Christianity. Not only was Jesus presented by Mohammed as one of the great prophets his predecessors, but the Virgin Birth of Jesus and his Second Advent are among the beliefs of Islam. We may therefore see the ironical situation that on certain points of the traditional Christian creed Mohammedans are more orthodox to-day than a large number of Protestant Christians. Yet in spite of these Christian elements in Islam, Mohammed seems to have known little of the teaching attributed to Jesus in the Gospels, and the *ethos* of the new religion was profoundly different from that of Christianity. It was much more like that of the militant Judaism of Maccabean days.

Mohammedanism soon spread victoriously over a good part of the old Roman Empire. Beside some of the Eastern provinces it won North Africa, and, for a time, much of Spain. The Byzantine Empire not only suffered constant pressure and loss from Northern Slavonic barbarians—these might wrest away Balkan countries for independent Slavonic kingdoms, yet they, at any rate, accepted the Orthodox faith—but on the East and South it had for eight centuries to carry on a fight, sometimes a victorious fight but on the whole a losing one, against the Moslem power. After the fall of Constantinople in 1453, the whole of Eastern Christianity—Orthodox and Monophysite, Greek, Coptic, Syriac, Armenian—was under the Moslem yoke, a set of communities tolerated indeed, but kept in a position of humiliation and contempt. It is not surprising that a Christianity which was the religion of old peoples enslaved and harassed did not show the same vigour of intellectual and cultural life as the Christianity which was the religion of the young, strong nations of the West. It was not till the rise of Russia that there was a Great Power in the world whose religion was Greek Orthodox. And the Russian Church was too much under State control, too fast-bound by tradition, to show much in the way of original religious thought: also the quality of the Russian educated class was not favourable to such a form of activity.

The only Christian thinker of European note produced by Russian Orthodox Christianity, the philosopher Vladimir Soloviev (1853–1900), in his last days drew near to the Roman communion. Leo Tolstoy (1828–1910) was not so much a thinker as a man of literary genius, possessed in the later period of life, prophet-wise, by certain ideas suggested to him by the Gospels, with which he constructed a form of religion of his own opposed to the religion of the Christian Church, though Tolstoy believed it to be the religion of Jesus. Tolstoy's religion has undoubtedly exercised wide influence upon Christian sentiment all the world over, though as a distinct form of religion it must now be practically extinct. If he has any prominent follower left, it is the Indian, Mahatma Gandhi, who professes a Tolstoyism blended with elements of the Hindu tradition.

Eastern Christianity as a whole has been distinguished from Western Christianity by the relatively greater prominence in it of asceticism. The monk and hermit and holy man have been more important figures in it than the bishop and priest. The extreme forms of self-torture, living for years on the top of a pillar, and so on, belong, as we have already noticed, to Eastern Christianity. To turn from the wearying transitoriness of earthly things to contemplation of the eternal and unchanging—that seems widely to have been felt in Eastern Christianity as the core, or the highest goal, of religion—renunciation and tranquillity, though

this is hardly anything distinctively Christian, but common to Eastern Christianity with Neoplatonism and Indian religion. Yet although Eastern Christianity has been intellectually sterile, it has certainly produced saints, men of an impressive personal holiness, whose inner life seems to be hidden in another world than this.

The situation of the Church in the West after the barbarian invasions was quite different from its situation in the old Roman Empire or in the Byzantine East. Instead of being confronted with a State embodying the traditions of an ancient civilization, in the shadow of which the Church itself had grown up, it was in contact with peoples still in a primitive stage of culture, only recently brought within the Christian fold, or still in process of being brought, for whom the Church embodied, not only the Christian life, but also all that survived of the old Græco-Roman civilization. The barbarian chieftains who established principalities over the area of Central and Western Europe had to turn to the Christian clergy not only for instruction in religion, but instruction in writing and law and scientific knowledge. They were as children before those who have the experience of riper years. Those churchmen who had been trained in the Church tradition were in somewhat the same position as European missionaries amongst primitive tribes to-day. The civilization of the old Mediterranean world had been an urban civilization, largely a sea-board civilization; in the early Middle Ages, it was a question of organizing Church work over large inland thinly-populated areas. The diocese of the medieval bishop was usually much larger than that of the old urban bishop.

The practical problems before the Church were now quite different from those which had confronted the members of small close societies surrounded by a pagan world, with which Christianity had begun. In such societies an intensity of enthusiastic life had been possible, which had largely made the imposition of fixed rules superfluous. The "fruits of the Spirit" had been love, joy and peace, and against such there was no law. Now widely spread multitudes of childish peoples, who all formally adhered to Christianity but were still in large part primitive men with violent unregulated impulses, had to be taught, so far as might be, to live as Christians. It was perhaps inevitable in such circumstances that Christianity should take on the form rather of a law, than of a Gospel—a body of hard-and-fast rules for children. If society was not to break up in chaos, all this mass of natural crude humanity must be under forcible government, and the Church authorities could hardly do anything but give the kings and chieftains their advice and co-operation. The Church thus entered into much closer association with the secular power than had been possible in the Roman Empire. This was especially the case in England before the Norman Conquest. "In no land was there such a blending of spiritual and temporal action as is seen in the Charter of Canute, where ealdormen and shire-bishops join in 'maintaining God's rights and my royal authority and the weal of all the people.'"[1] "The distinction between spiritual and temporal authorization was very little drawn" (Stubbs). On the Continent, in the "Holy Roman Empire" established by Charlemagne (A.D. 800), the Emperors of German race found in the Church the means of spreading through their dominion a uniform culture with Christian characteristics.

Since, however, in regard to secular government, Western and Central Europe was divided amongst a number of separate kingdoms and principalities, the close association between the Church authorities and each secular power entailed an obvious danger of the One Church becoming similarly divided, falling into a multitude of different local Churches or national Churches. Against this tendency, the principle of the Unity of Christendom was represented by the Bishop of Rome. In relation to the Roman See, all Western Churches everywhere were connected with one centre and recognized one authority overriding all local distinctions. Amid the centrifugal tendencies in the Europe of the Middle Ages the importance of keeping Christendom together as one gave the Pope a position he had never had in the old Roman Empire.

[1] Sir Lewis Dibdin and A. L. Smith in the *Report* of the Archbishop's Committee on Church and State (S.P.C.K., 1917).

No doubt in this case too what happened cannot be accounted for only by the circumstances of the time; the personalities of individual men who arose at the critical moments also determined the result. Men like Gregory I ("the Great," a member of the old Roman aristocracy, who was Pope from 590 to 604), and Gregory VII (Hildebrand, Pope from 1073 to 1085), counted for a great deal in gaining recognition all over Western Christendom for the Papal claims. It was generally understood from the beginning of the Middle Ages that local disputes in any part of Europe could be carried to Rome for decision by the supreme spiritual authority. This appellate jurisdiction—the power of declaring in a particular case what the existing law required—was not in itself the power to make new laws. But the idea that the Pope had legislative authority as well was current quite early in the Middle Ages and was definitely established in the great code of Canon Law compiled by Gratian of Bologna in the middle of the twelfth century. "Canon Law" is Church Law—the rules for the behaviour of Christian people, especially rules concerning the clergy, derived partly from old custom in the Church, partly from decrees of Councils, partly from Papal enactments.

The close concurrence of all these different kinds of authority—that of the Pope, that of secular emperors and kings, that of smaller principalities and cities, that of the local bishops and clergy, that of established custom—inevitably, human nature being what it is, led to continual friction and quarrels. Of such quarrels the history of the Middle Ages is full. The greatest struggle of all was that between the Popes and the Hohenstaufen Emperors, Frederick I Barbarossa (1152–89), Henry VI (1190–7) and Frederick II (1212–50). It was the general view that the Holy Roman Empire, properly co-extensive with Christendom, had two heads, one for religion, the Pope, and one for secular affairs, the Emperor. The "two swords" spoken of in Luke xxii. 38, were explained as an allegory of the two divine authorities exercised by these two Powers. The adherents of the Emperor, nicknamed "Ghibellines" (those of the Pope were called "Guelphs"), maintained that the Popes sought to extend their authority illegitimately into the Emperor's province. Dante (1265–1321) was an ardent believer in the view that the salvation of Christian society was to be found in the reassertion of the Emperor's authority over Christendom, and in the two Powers each keeping strictly to its own sphere.

For all the power which the Church had in the Middle Ages, it did not think of changing the fixed institutions of the world to remodel them in a realm of communal brotherhood, from which forcible coercion and war were banished, any more now than it had done under the old Empire. With this mass of crude humanity which bore the Christian name but was only very partially Christian in spirit, to have attempted to rule without force would have meant giving up the weak as a prey to the violent. The Church still held to the view which it had adopted under the Roman Empire long before, that a state of the world in which there was war and inequality and forcible coercion was not the ideal state, but that it was the only state possible for fallen Man, and it was a state which would soon pass away with the end of the present world. Yet it strove, even in the present state, to realize a unity of Christendom, an organic society of men, distributed in a system of fixed classes according to function and vocation,[1] held together by a common faith, a common obedience to the one divinely-appointed spiritual authority, and certain common principles of conduct in public and private life. Of course, even that was very imperfectly realized, but it was an ideal which was always there and did to some extent influence the course of the actual world. And meantime a kind of life nearer, it was thought, to the Christian ideal, went on being exhibited in the monastic societies.

War between Christians necessarily involves wickedness and injustice on one side or the other,

[1] The idea of "vocation" in secular life, the belief that a man can reach the highest degree of sanctity while following some occupation in the world, is often claimed by Protestants to be a new idea brought in by Luther and the Reformation. This claim, says one of our chief Protestant authorities in this field, is "definitely false." The idea is already formulated in Medieval Catholicism. Troeltsch, *Soziallehren*, p. 314.

often on both. But the Catholic Church has never asserted that the suppression of public wrong by force was un-Christian; it has never asserted that a Christian was untrue to his profession, if he bore arms, even though it was against fellow-Christians, in a just public quarrel. In fact, the Roman Church has precluded itself for ever from taking such a view by having declared Joan of Arc a saint. And if a Christian might fight in battle against fellow-Christians, to rectify public wrong, much more might he fight against non-Christians to rectify wrongs done to the Christian body as a whole. On such a principle a war in which the Christian peoples combined to rescue the holy places of Palestine from the Moslems—a Crusade—was proclaimed by the Popes to be not only legitimate, but a work of high merit. The Crusades are a dramatic episode in medieval history. In a way they were no doubt an expression of the unity of Christendom. Some of those who took part in them represented the type of Christian warrior in a shining way, like Saint Louis of France, or the Knight in Chaucer's *Canterbury Tales*, but they also swept along with them a torrent of mere ruffianism to the East. If to-day it is sad for Christians to see one of the greatest monuments of early Christian art, the Church of Saint Sophia at Constantinople, in drear disfigurement as a mosque, it has to be remembered that the first desecration and despoilment of that wonderful building was perpetrated by the Latin Crusaders in 1204.

Many people to-day are repelled from the Roman Catholic Church by its seeming to treat its members too much as children, dictating times and petty rules for their devotions, limiting their liberty of thought and inquiry, giving the priest a right of interference in intimate domestic details and points of personal conduct. Whether it is true or not that the Roman Church controls the lives of its members in a way which modern men rightly refuse to endure, it has to be remembered that the Roman system, with all its rules and devotional practices, was actually formed in the first instance for peoples on the childish level. Its use of images, for instance, began in the idea of making masses of people who could not read familiar with the sacred story and its characters, just as the religious education of children often begins with Bible picture-books.

A bishop of Marseilles, about 600 A.D., found his flock offering homage to pictures in a church and had them destroyed. He was censured for this action by Pope Gregory I. "That you forbade homage to be offered to the pictures," the Pope wrote, "we wholly approve, but you did wrong in destroying them. For the unlearned and for the heathen a picture takes the place of a book." Later on, when the practice of asking the prayers of saints in heaven, and especially those of the Mother of the Lord, became common, the custom of offering homage to their images also came in. The theological theory was that the image had no virtue in itself but was simply a help enabling the Christian to address his act of reverence to his exalted fellow-Christian in heaven with fuller mental realization, just as the Royal Standard may be saluted as an act of reverence to the King.

Or again, the penetration of priestly control into the intimate life of each individual member of the community, secured by the obligatory practice of private confession at fixed times to a priest, was an outcome of that general control exercised by the community over the conduct of its members in primitive times, when each community was a small group of people who knew each other, and a member who fell into sin made public confession before the congregation. Now, when all the people scattered over a large area professed Christianity and were still in the condition of children, that help in the struggle with primitive impulse which each member had got in early times by opening up his inner life to the community had to be got by his opening it up to the representative of the community, the priest.[1]

The Middle Ages fell very far short of their ideal; there was plenty of brutality and practical unbelief all through what is sometimes called the "age of faith." There was a great deal of evil even in the highest places of the Church. Some of the Popes were exceed-

[1] The Liberal Protestant A. Harnack described as "culpable (*sträfliche*) folly" the procedure of the Protestant Reformation in "tearing up by its roots the whole tree of Confession," because certain of its fruits were rotten. *Reden und Aufsätze*, II (1904), p. 257.

ingly bad men. But the Christian life continued to show itself, and by no means as only a simple keeping of rules. Self-sacrificing charity and ardent devotion broke out spontaneously over and over again. Notable examples are the kindled feeling in the writings of St. Bernard (1091–1153), and the creation by St. Francis of Assisi (1182–1226) of his new order of barefoot friars who went about among men, showing radiant happiness in poverty. The order of St. Dominic, founded at the same time, although its early record is somewhat shadowed by its connexion with the savage persecution of heretics, also produced great Christian preachers and thinkers.

It was during the last four centuries of the Middle Ages (from the middle of the eleventh to the middle of the fifteenth) that its great works were produced. Society was becoming more civilized; men were growing up from the childish state; knowledge was increasing. Those centuries have left monuments in a great Christian Art, seen in the Romanesque and Gothic cathedrals; in the Scholastic Philosophy wherein thought laboured, not unfruitfully, to combine Christian beliefs in one reasonable system with large elements taken over from Plato and Aristotle, the philosophy whose chief exponent is the Dominican, St. Thomas of Aquinum (1227–74); and lastly in Dante's *Divina Commedia*, one of the great poems in the heritage of mankind.

The mystical stream which had come into

Christianity from Neoplatonism through the fifth-century writer who pretended to be Dionysius the Areopagite, a disciple of St. Paul, and who succeeded in imposing upon the whole of medieval Christendom, entered into various combinations with the authentic Christian tradition. Throughout the Middle Ages this stream continued to break out in individual writers —in John the Scot (in those days a "Scot" meant an Irishman!) who died at Oxford about 886,[1] in Heinrich Eckhart, a Dominican (died in 1329), in the two other Dominican monks, Heinrich Suso (1295–1365) and Johann Tauler (about 1300–61), in Mother Julian of Norwich (about 1343–1443). In the case of the first two the Neoplatonic element preponderated over the Christian: Eckhart was condemned after his death by the Pope. Even the "Mystical Theology" which the Church has approved is largely derived in the last resort from pagan Neoplatonism through the fraudulent writings just mentioned. Its questionable origins do not, of course, necessarily invalidate the doctrines it contains or the experiences connected with them, though they may suggest caution to those who imagine that mysticism is the highest thing, or the most essential thing, in Christianity. In Mother Julian simpler and purer Christian feeling welled up and found expression winning by its naturalness and *naïveté*. But when Mother Julian wrote Christian Europe was already on the eve of a great transformation.

[1] Sometimes called Scotus Erigena ("Erin-born").

CHAPTER VIII

THE REFORMATION

THE Reformation in the sixteenth century was by far the most momentous event in the history of Christianity since the conversion of the Roman Empire. The cleavage it made in the Christian world was more important than the division between Latin Catholicism and Greek Orthodoxy, inasmuch as the Eastern Churches separated from Rome were Churches among peoples either subject to alien Moslem rule or semi-barbarous like the old Russians, whereas the Churches separated from Rome by the Reformation were those of the northern peoples who were destined, in Europe, in America and in Australasia, to become the most powerful and materially civilized on the globe. The Reformers repudiated large parts of the Catholic tradition, but they added nothing considerable to it. Their positive teaching consisted of parts of the Catholic tradition which they retained: their difference from the Roman Church was negative. A Protestant may admit this without prejudice to the Reformation. He may say that the work of clearing away all the false accretions which had gathered round the primitive Christian faith brought in fact a great positive gain, just as the cleaning of a picture or the freeing of a bronze statue from a crust may allow a beauty to reappear which had become effaced. The Catholic on the other hand may say that, even if the doctrines of Protestants were bits of Catholic teaching, by being separated from the other Catholic doctrines, which Protestants rejected, they were set in a false light which made them, so isolated, actually misleading.

No doubt various motives entered into the great movement initiated by Martin Luther when he nailed his ninety-five theses to the church-door in Wittenberg (October 31, 1517). All instructed Roman Catholics admit that life in the Church had sunk at that moment to a low level, that the sale of indulgences, which was the immediate occasion of Luther's protest, was a horrible abuse, and that had Luther's violence and self-assurance (as they consider) not carried him to the lengths they did, he might have been the agent of a bitterly needed reform. Behind the sixteenth-century Reformers there was a movement of mind in the Christian world which had been working for some time towards the same end as theirs— a movement shown in such figures as Wycliffe and Huss a century earlier. It arose from a sense of the contrast between the Christianity exhibited in the New Testament and contemporary Catholicism. Here again, instructed Catholics would not deny that such a contrast existed; they would only maintain that the later Catholicism was either a legitimate development of the religion which the New Testament shows still in germ under conditions quite different from those of later days, or a decline in practice which did not impair the truth of Catholic doctrine so far as authoritatively defined.

Before any individual to whom the contrast in question seemed to prove current Catholicism to be wrong could engage upon active opposition to the ecclesiastical authorities he had, of course, to be convinced of his right to act upon his own individual judgment. The right of private judgment thus became a fundamental idea in the Reformation, and the essence of the whole movement is sometimes presented as an assertion of spiritual freedom against the claim of a Church to dictate what a man is to do and to believe. Like most popular notions, this has a measure of truth in it together with some confusion. There are two wholly different senses in which a religious community may tell an individual what he is to do and believe. It may declare that these are the practices and beliefs essential to membership in the community: if an individual wishes to adhere to the community he can do so only on the condition of accepting them; if he already belongs to the community and repudiates them he will be ejected: there is nothing tyrannous in this, provided that a man's adherence to a community is purely voluntary. Or the religious community may have the power to inflict pains and penalties upon individuals, whether they wish to belong to the community or not, and it may punish in that way everyone who in action or belief asserts his independence. This is tyranny, and it is a kind of tyranny which the Church certainly exercised in the sixteenth century. It cannot, however, be said that the Reformers stood for the principle of complete religious toleration. Perhaps, in view of the numerous *autos-da-fè* perpetrated at the bidding of the Roman Catholic ecclesiastics, too much has been made of the particular case in which the Protestant authorities of Geneva burnt Servetus because of his theories about the Trinity (October 27, 1553), but the important thing was the general belief behind this Protestant *auto-da-fè* (not the only one), that although it was right to deny great parts of the Catholic tradition, you might not deny other parts without becoming liable to death. That it was right to put heretics to death Luther himself declared. Of the Jews Luther said:

> " Their synagogues ought to be razed to the ground, their houses destroyed, their books, including the Talmud, and even the Old Testament, taken from them, and their Rabbis compelled to earn their bread by hard labour."

" The right of the civil magistrate to punish heresy was maintained by the Helvetic, Scottish, Belgic and Saxon Confessions." [1]

Cranmer and Ridley, who were themselves

[1] Lecky, *Rationalism in Europe*, Chapter IV.

burnt at the stake as heretics, had taken an active part in the persecution of Anabaptists.

It is remarkable how much of the Catholic tradition the principal Reformers retained. They retained the Creeds of the Church which formulated the faith as taught by the Œcumenical Councils of the fourth and fifth centuries, and in this way they were bound fast to the Catholic doctrine of the Trinity and the two natures of Christ. They retained belief in the Fall and in the Augustinian view of the transmission to all men of original sin, which made them liable to eternal damnation apart from any sins they might individually commit.[1] They retained belief in the Atonement wrought by the Blood of Jesus. They retained, finally, belief that the New Testament writings of infallible inspiration were precisely the twenty-seven which had been marked off by the Church's tradition, and no others. In regard to the Old Testament, the Reformers rejected the books which were not regarded as inspired by the Jews, those, that is to say, which constitute the Apocrypha, and which were either written in Greek or survived only in a Greek translation from the lost

[1] See Article IX of the Church of England. "Original Sin standeth not in the following of *Adam* (as the *Pelagians* do vainly talk); but it is the fault and corruption of the Nature of every man, that naturally is ingendered of the offspring of *Adam*; whereby man is very far gone from original righteousness, and is of his own nature inclined to evil, so that the flesh lusteth always contrary to the spirit; and therefore in every person born into this world, it deserveth God's wrath and damnation."

Hebrew or Aramaic originals. Here again they added no book to the Church's Bible, and only cut out some which were included in it.

The Church's New Testament and the Jews' Old Testament formed the Bible upon which Protestantism in the sixteenth century was built up—the impregnable rock, Protestants believed, of God's Word. So long as this belief continued, Protestants, although they had left the ground of Roman doctrine, could not wander far from it. Individual interpretation of the infallible scriptures might lead to a certain diversity of belief, but the range of difference was limited by the necessity of deriving all belief with an appearance of reasonableness from one fixed form of words, dictated, both Catholics and Protestants agreed, by the Holy Spirit.

In two ways mainly the Christianity of the New Testament seemed to the Reformers to differ from Roman Catholicism. One was its relative simplicity, in contrast with that ecclesiastical apparatus of sacerdotal hierarchy, miraculous sacraments, monastic asceticism, invocation of saints, images, holy water, medals, relics, rosaries. The other way was that the temper of Christianity in the New Testament seemed to be one of exuberant joy in a salvation already possessed by faith, while that of Roman Catholicism seemed a painful and anxious striving to win by an accumulation of meritorious works a salvation doubtful up to the end of life on earth.

In regard to the mass of Roman Catholic institutions and customs impugned by the Reformers, as not found in the New Testament, they fall, from the Roman Catholic standpoint, into two distinct categories. Some—images and invocation of saints for example—Roman Catholics would admit to be absent from the New Testament; but they would maintain that they were a legitimate development in the life of the Church and were consonant in principle with New Testament religion. In the case of others, Roman Catholics would maintain against Protestants that they *were* found in the New Testament—apostolic orders, the primacy of St. Peter, sacraments of supernatural character. And those in the sixteenth century who broke away from the Roman communion differed considerably, one group from another, in the extent to which they went in repudiating existing Roman Catholic institutions and customs. The Church of England retained some which were repudiated by all other reformed bodies. It retained the three ecclesiastical orders of bishops, priests, and deacons, and claims that these orders have been transmitted in the manner which makes them, according to the Catholic theory, valid. This Rome denies, but the disagreement turns mainly upon a question of historical evidence, what precisely happened in the case of Archbishop Parker. The old parish system went on in England as before the Reformation with an unbroken succession of priests officiating in the old stone churches. How far the Church of England has gone in repudiating other Roman Catholic institutions and customs it is impossible to state precisely, because the queer thing about the Church of England is that it allows a diversity of opinion amongst its official teachers wider than any other Christian body does, except perhaps the Congregationalists. The extreme High Church wing of the Church of England has retained practically all the impugned Roman institutions and customs, except that it does not acknowledge the supremacy of the Pope *in the Roman sense* and uses the common liturgy in the vernacular. The extreme Low Church or "Evangelical" wing repudiates all the impugned Roman institutions and customs and differs from Presbyterian or Calvinist Protestantism only in so far as its inclusion in the Church of England obliges it to acquiesce in a fixed liturgy incorporating traditional Catholic prayers, in a minimum of vestments—a surplice and stole worn by the officiating minister—and in the system of three orders transmitted in the way prescribed by Catholic tradition, though it explains that it regards the system as one purely of convenience, not as essential to the life of the Church. Yet those who present these widely-diverging forms of belief and practice are included in one ecclesiastical organization under the direction of one body of bishops. Perhaps that faculty of the English for acquiescing in illogical makeshifts which has enabled them throughout their history to surmount successfully so many practical difficulties is nowhere seen more signally than in the Anglican Church. Yet sometimes logic gets its revenge on those who go on disregarding it.

Of the other Reformed Churches, the Lutherans retained a doctrine of the Eucharist which, though not theologically identical with the Roman doctrine, resembled it in asserting that the "substance" of Christ was present in the consecrated elements: they also retained the use of the crucifix in churches. Other Reformed bodies denied that any real change took place in the bread and wine used in Communion, and regarded all sacred images as a breach of the Second Commandment. Baptism and Communion in bread and wine, since the New Testament states them to have been instituted by Jesus, were retained by all the Reformed Churches, till George Fox in the seventeenth century founded the Society of Friends, which went further than any other body in rejecting traditional forms of organization and worship, maintaining that the statements in the New Testament about Baptism and the Eucharist were to be understood purely as figures of speech. In proportion as a Rationalist temper has prevailed in Protestantism, there has naturally been an unwillingness to admit any supernatural character in the two sacraments, and in so far as such Protestantism felt itself in former generations bound to the New Testament, it asserted hotly against Rome that the New Testament writers were not to be construed as implying any such thing. To-day a change has taken place. The prevalent opinion among Continental critics now is that St. Paul and the writer of the Fourth Gospel did believe that Christ was really and substantially taken into the person of him who partook of the consecrated bread and wine, as Catholics have always maintained. Modern critical Protestants are free to admit this, because they no longer feel bound to believe everything which St. Paul and St. John believed: the New Testament writers shared, we are now told, many primitive illusions still rife in their world.

The controversy between Catholics and Protestants in regard to all the practices not exhibited, or not clearly exhibited, in the New Testament has been much complicated by the fact that popular practice in Catholicism has often not corresponded strictly with authorized theological theory. Catholic theologians, for instance, may lay down that no virtue resides in an image, that to address an act of homage to it is a purely symbolical way of expressing the reverence felt for the invisible person the image represents—Jesus or Mary or some Christian hero now in the Divine presence: in actual practice it can hardly be questioned that Roman Catholic image-worship has sometimes differed little from the ancient idolatry. The old Greek philosophers too had a theory, analogous to the Roman Catholic theory, which justified their idolatry as symbolical. Again, the practice of the invocation of saints in heaven may be shown to be consonant with New Testament ideas of intercession. The common Protestant argument, that Jesus is the One Mediator, is clearly wide of the mark, since if that meant that a Christian should not ask the prayers of anyone but Jesus, it would rule out his asking the prayers of a living fellow Christian—a practice which the New Testament sanctions. The question at issue is whether death makes such a difference that, although it was right for a Christian to ask the prayers of, let us say, St. Francis when St. Francis was alive, it became wrong to do so from the moment that St. Francis passed into the Divine presence.[1] But it is possible to allow that to ask the intercession of saints is in itself nothing irreconcilable with New Testament religion, and yet to hold that the worship of saints in popular Catholicism has in practice often differed little from polytheism. Or again, the value attached to relics may be shown to be the same in principle with

[1] Nothing is said in the New Testament about asking the prayers of saints of heaven ; but the New Testament makes two statements from which the rightness of the practice might seem logically to follow : (1) that the saints are " with Christ " ; (2) that Christ is continually engaged in intercession for his members upon earth. To be with a person and not share his main interest is a poor mode of proximity. Nothing is said in the New Testament about the baptism of infants, nor about the keeping of Sunday, yet a large number of Protestants think that the former practice, and practically all old-fashioned Protestants think that the latter practice, may be justified by inferential argument from one or two New Testament phrases. A much stronger case for asking the prayers of the saints in heaven can be made out on the same principle.

the belief, vouched for by the New Testament, that the sick were cured by "handkerchiefs or aprons" carried away from the body of St. Paul (Acts xix. 12), or with the healing of a woman by her touching the hem of Jesus' garment. If a material object, it may be argued, from its connexion with a holy man's body can convey such virtue, is it to be thought that the virtue evaporates after a definite time or ceases at the holy man's death? As a matter of fact, most modern Protestant critics would here too agree with Catholics that the belief in such New Testament cures and belief in relics was of one piece; but they would regard all such belief as equally superstitious. In practice, at any rate, to many observers the cult of relics in popular Catholicism has seemed to differ little from primitive fetishism.

It has been authoritatively admitted on the Catholic side that the danger of such practices lapsing into superstition in popular religion is a real one, and it would not be denied that in many places popular Catholicism has sunk low. Catholics would only urge that Protestants were wrong in condemning the use because of the abuse. The right course is not to abandon good things because they are abused, but to try by more efficient instruction to prevent the abuse; and this duty, they would say, is specially laid upon Catholic parish priests, though they may not all perform it properly or successfully. Against this on the Protestant side it may be argued that Catholicism cannot get all the credit for its ideal and treat the gap between ideal and practice as irrelevant in regard to its general valuation. Practices which so easily lapse into superstitition are condemned by that very liability. It will be seen that here is matter for dispute without end. Much of the old controversial literature seems to us now a beating of the air. Many Christians to-day of the Reformed Churches would approach a consideration of the impugned Catholic practices with a wider outlook than Protestants of the sixteenth and seventeenth centuries, a larger knowledge of psychology, a less servile attachment to the letter of the New Testament, and a greater readiness to admit variations in Christian practice according to differences of place and time. Fair-minded Roman Catholics, on the other hand, would admit that Protestants had some ground for disgust with many things actually presented to their eyes by popular Catholicism in its lower forms.

The second great difference which Luther found between New Testament Christianity and contemporary Catholicism was that while St. Paul rejoiced, and taught his converts to rejoice, in a salvation already possessed by faith, Roman Catholics represented salvation as something to be won by good works, of which a man could never be sure that he had done enough. This was the great controversy regarding "justification by faith alone" which was regarded as the most fundamental of the distinctive "Evangelical" doctrines, and which has filled libraries of theological debate. It was a controversy on the same field as that between Augustine and the Pelagians centuries before; indeed Luther expressly appealed to Augustine, and contended that the trouble with contemporary Catholicism was that it had become in effect Pelagian.[1] The New Testament spoke both of a part played by human will in man's salvation and of salvation as won for man by the work of Christ and bestowed by the Grace of God. "Work out your own salvation, for it is God that worketh in you." We have seen that Catholicism, since the time of Augustine, had committed itself to the doctrine that there was no movement toward good in the soul of man which was not due to God's Grace; at the same time Catholicism habitually spoke of the "merit" of good works performed by the human will acting under the influence of Divine Grace. It asserted both together the reality of human voluntary choice, and the inability of man to do any good work except by Divine Grace working in him. While the ground of man's salvation, the Atonement wrought by Christ, was a Divine action to whose virtue sinners contributed nothing, in the in-

[1] Perhaps the charge was not inexcusable. "The acutely twice-born type is . . . in the New Testament represented by St. Paul . . .; and thenceforward, in the Christian Churches, it is carried on, not by the common Catholic stream, which in the long run is obstinately 'semi-Pelagian,' but largely by St. Augustine, and more emphatically still by Luther and Calvin, the Jansenists, and the Puritans." Baron F. von Hügel, *The Reality of God* (1931), p. 214.

dividual appropriation of that salvation man's will came into play all through, though in some inexplicable way all the time man owed his will for good to the Grace of God. The Reformers likewise asserted that man's salvation on the one side was due to the work of Christ and the action of Divine Grace, and on the other side implied an action of the human will in accepting the Divine gift and directing itself to good works. Catholics and Protestants, that is to say, both asserted both of two apparently incompatible things: the difference was one of emphasis. For if both things are true, you may lay the main stress on one or other of them, and according as you do, a different type of religion results. Luther and the Reformers laid the main stress on the work of Christ and the saving Grace of God. Looking at these things, away from his own imperfect performance, a man may feel confident that his sins are forgiven, that God already wills nothing in regard to him but good; he may rejoice in a salvation he possesses already. Contemporary Catholicism, considering that numbers of men did fail to attain salvation because of defects of their will, laid its main stress on the effort which man should make to bring his will into the right adjustment to God's by acting in accordance with God's commandments and by methodical self-discipline—most effectively by monastic self-discipline. And no doubt when a man's attention is turned to his own performance the result may be humbling rather than exhilarating. In controversy, as was natural, each side misrepresented the other. Catholics habitually spoke as if the Reformed doctrine of justification by faith alone meant that, according to the Reformers, man could be saved without an adjustment of his will to God's in practice, though Protestants always maintained that such an adjustment was the natural consequence of faith, and that where it was absent the supposed faith was not genuine. Protestants habitually spoke as if the Catholic insistence upon good works meant a denial of the value of Christ's work and the idea that man could perform good works in his own strength without God's Grace, or that man could by his good works put God into his debt —an idea which the term " merits " used by Catholics unhappily suggests.

From ancient and medieval Catholic prayers phrases may be culled which assert, as strongly as Protestants have ever asserted, the utter dependence of man in all his good works upon Divine Grace : " O Lord God, who seest that we put not our trust in anything that we do " —" Almighty God, who seest that we have no power of ourselves to help ourselves "— " Because through the weakness of our mortal nature we can do no good thing without thee, grant us the help of thy grace "—" We who cannot have any being without thee " —" Forasmuch as without thee we are not able to please thee," etc. It is again established Catholic doctrine that the moment any sinner turns to God in an act of real repentance and faith he receives the Divine forgiveness, like Manfred in Dante, who had lived an evil life up to the moment when he found himself at point of death on the field of battle, pierced by two mortal wounds. Then, he is made to say, "I yielded myself weeping to Him who pardons willingly: my sins had been horrible; but the Divine Goodness has so large arms that every being who turns to it it receives" (*Purgatorio*, iii, 119–122). In one moment Manfred is safe in those arms, although he has done no good work upon earth and will never have the opportunity of doing one. The idea that man has to purchase God's goodwill by actions of his own is thoroughly opposed to Catholic doctrine. Yet it is an idea which comes very easily to men conscious of their own unworthiness, and although in the Catholic liturgies the prevenience of God's Grace is, as we have just seen, frequently asserted, phrases in a liturgy may remain conventional forms without much power to shape men's thoughts in practical life. When therefore Luther asserted that the great multitude of those who in his own day subjected themselves to an ascetic rule, as monks and nuns, thought of God's good will as something which they must win in that way, the fact that there were those phrases in the traditional liturgy does not prove him to have been wrong. The joy in a salvation already possessed had really been a note of primitive Christianity. It can hardly be shown to have been in the same way a note of popular Catholicism in the sixteenth century. And, allowing all the blemishes which have been pointed out in the character of Luther—the grossness and immorality of some of his utterances on conjugal relations, the occasional brutality of his language, the impulsive inaccuracy of some of his statements on matters of fact—it may still be true that he was a man of great heart and (in some respects) great spiritual discernment. It may still be true that his religious genius made him detect, below the particular abuses of contemporary Catholicism, what was profoundly wrong in its attitude to God. Further, there was something about this big, imperfect man of such a kind that what he felt shook the hearts of thousands in Europe, broke up the crust of existing things, and changed the face of the world.

It has often been found that by directing the main attention to the Divine action—to the work of Christ, to the Grace of God—Evangelical religion has produced in response a temper of love and gratitude, from which the new mode of conduct has sprung spontaneously.[1] When

[1] A prominent Evangelical preacher of the nineteenth century, through whom a remarkable number of lives were permanently changed, gave it as his experience that his preaching was far less successful in bringing about conversions when it took the form of a call to repentance (speaking as it were in the imperative mood), than when it was a setting forth of the love of God in Christ (the indicative mood). As has been already remarked in this volume, the distinctive thing in Christianity is rather a new announcement than a new command, a " Gospel " rather than a Law.

such religion has spoken of the delusion of doing good works in order to merit God's goodwill, "deadly doing," etc., it has never meant to imply that a man could go on living in deliberate sin and enjoy an assurance of salvation by faith: it has always been taken as understood that the reception of salvation by faith implied a right direction of the will. Though one ought not perhaps to say "never." Luther and Melanchthon did on one occasion encourage a dissolute German prince, whose help they needed, to live on the sly in bigamy; yet that action of the Reformer's has been generally recognized by Protestants to be one of the great blots on his career, and it cannot be taken as representing the genuine Protestant doctrine.[1] Only, if a disproportionate emphasis on the part of the human will in man's salvation has sometimes led to a legalistic impoverishment of the Christian life in Catholicism, Catholics may point with justice to the case of Luther and Philip of Hesse as indicating that an insistence upon trust in God's goodwill which gives insufficient emphasis to the part of the human will in obedience is not without its dangers.

It should perhaps be pointed out, to obviate

[1] A phrase once used by Luther in a letter "Pecca fortiter" ("Sin courageously") has probably been unfairly urged against him. The letter is written to some one who is distressed because of his many failings and may mean no more than "Although you find yourself repeatedly lapsing from the Christian ideal of conduct, do not lose heart"—expressed in Luther's characteristic slapdash, vigorous, picturesque, but often incautious and unfortunate, way.

misunderstanding, that when Protestants spoke of the assurance of a salvation already possessed, they did not necessarily mean that no man who possessed such a salvation could ever lose it again by his own turning away from God. Catholics maintained that it was always possible for anyone in a state of salvation to fall away by his own wilfulness or negligence, and that a man should never relax his vigilance against such declension up to the moment of his death. On this question Protestants were divided: the Calvinists, consistently with their one-sided emphasis on God's Will in man's salvation, denied that any of the elect after they had been led to conversion could ever fall away again: other Evangelicals, looking at the part played by man's will, taught, like the Catholics, that falling away was possible. Even those who in other respects formed a single group amongst Evangelicals might be divided on this question: amongst the Methodists, for instance, Whitefield, whose views were Calvinist, denied the possibility of any really saved person falling away; John Wesley asserted it. Probably the question will not be solved by argument till the deeper problem of reconciling rationally the relative actions of the Divine and the human will has been solved; and that is never. According as one looks at either the Divine or the human will in isolation, a contrary inference results. Looking at the former, one may argue that the Divine Shepherd will never lose again the sheep He has brought home;

looking at the latter, one may argue that the same misuse of free will which in some cases prevents a man from ever receiving God's salvation in other cases may lead to a man's throwing it away after he has received it. Since Christianity teaches that both the apparently contradictory aspects are true, an inference drawn from one alone is plainly insecure; the right inference from their interaction could be drawn only by some one who had a rational understanding of that interaction. So long as that is mysterious, the question whether salvation, once possessed, can be lost, must remain unanswerable.

Apart, however, from the particular differences which distinguished the Reformed teaching from that of Rome, perhaps the most important difference which the Reformation made was the repudiation in itself by the vigorous Protestant peoples of the authority of the Pope and the Roman theological system. So far as Rome in those days called in material force, wherever the Governments of States were amenable to its direction, in order to suppress the utterance of views differing from those it authorized, we may think of this breaking away of Protestant States from the Roman allegiance as a movement to religious freedom. Even if opinion was not really free in sixteenth-century England and in Protestant States generally, still the rulers of these States did not enforce religion of the Roman pattern; so that, as a consequence of the Reformation, varieties of Christianity could

come into being and show what they were worth, which would have had little chance of surviving, if Rome had continued to dominate Europe. This was a fact of immense consequence for subsequent European history. Of course the fact may be differently estimated. From the standpoint of those who believe that the Papal claim to decisive authority in matters of faith and morals was founded on the provision expressly made by Jesus Christ himself, the living Head of the Church, for the guidance of his Church when his own visible presence was withdrawn, the breaking away of dissentient communities was wholly lamentable; Roman Catholics can emphasize the setback to the cause of Christ in the world which has come from disunion; discordant bodies each trying a way of its own; no central direction; no agreement in witness before the non-Christian world; sad disintegration such as was inevitable, once men left the Divine plan to follow their own fancies. On the other hand, those who do not believe that Jesus has ever conferred upon the Bishops of Rome the authority claimed see in the formation of those Christian bodies independent of Rome a great liberation. The disunion of Christendom they would admit to be an evil; but disagreement is an evil almost inseparable from freedom. The ideal unity at which they aim would not be a unity imposed by authority, but a unity arrived at by men who severally follow truth according to their free judgments and find that at the end of the quest they meet.

And the unity so attained might be one rich in varieties; for not all varieties are discordant. It might prove that the divided Christian bodies had each stood for some part of the truth which it apprehended more vividly than the rest did, and when that part of the truth was freed from the distortions and errors which now make variety mean conflict, it might prove that each of these bodies had brought its distinctive contribution to the life of the universal Church.

If one considers the type of Christianity constituted by Protestantism in the sixteenth century as a whole, one may see its chief weakness to have been the inner self-contradiction by which it declared on principle Catholic tradition to be liable to error, to be actually in many points erroneous, and at the same time took one bit of Catholic tradition as its fundamental dogma, which might not be questioned —the infallibility of a particular collection of writings. The appeal to scripture against the teaching of the Church might indeed be logical as an *argumentum ad hominem*. Catholics have sometimes urged against Protestants, "How can you set the Bible against the Church, when it is after all only from the Church that you have got the Bible?" But if a messenger comes bringing a verbal message, and at the same time delivers in confirmation of this message a document in writing which he affirms to be a genuine letter of the person from whom the message purports to come, and if on examining the document I find its statements incompatible with the messenger's verbal statements, I can logically use the document *against the messenger*, to convict him of being untrustworthy. I should be illogical only if for other purposes I built upon a document of whose authenticity I had no guarantee but an untrustworthy messenger's word, if I used it as evidence in my dealings with other people. Whether there is in truth an incompatibility between the teaching of the New Testament and the teaching of the Roman Catholic Church this is not the place to inquire; *if* there is such an incompatibility, Protestants were not illogical in adducing it to convict the Roman Church on its own ground. But they did more than this. They built up their own theology upon the New Testament as the infallible word of God, while the only ground they had for regarding this particular set of writings as specially inspired was the Church's tradition, which in other instances they repudiated as fallible. That was the weakness in the structure of old-fashioned Protestantism, which has brought it in our day to ruin.

CHAPTER IX

FROM THE REFORMATION TO THE FRENCH REVOLUTION

It was a new Europe which the Reformation left divided into two separate groups, the nations predominantly Roman Catholic on one side, and on the other side national States in which the majority, adopting one or other form of Protestantism, had severed themselves from the Roman Communion. It was new, not only on account of the Reformation, but on account of the whole movement of mind in the fifteenth and sixteenth centuries which we call the Renaissance. The result of this fresh contact with the pre-Christian culture of the Græco-Roman world through its surviving monuments, literary and artistic, was to detach masses of men in all European countries not only from the Roman Communion, as the Reformation did, but from Christianity altogether. The invention of printing and multiplication of printed books amongst the people at large was a factor of great importance in promoting the expression of thought. Politics, philosophic and scientific inquiry, art, which had been more or less controlled by religion, by Christianity, became secularized. It is this process of secularization, with its consequences, happy or unhappy, which marks off the European world since the Renaissance, as the "Modern World," from the Middle Ages.

In European politics the secularization was conspicuous. Men still cared enough about theology in the first part of the seventeenth century for the antagonism between Roman Catholic and Reformed either to be a main ground of wars, as in the case of the terrible Thirty Years War which devastated Germany (1618–48), or to add intensity to quarrels arising on other grounds. Yet the medieval idea of a united Christendom gave place after the Renaissance to the idea of the separate secular State, dynastic or national, basing its whole conduct on its own separate worldly interests. Machiavelli (1469–1527) with his hard and brilliant, completely cynical and pagan, political philosophy was the voice of the new age. Europe became a group of States for each of which "sacred egoism" was its supreme law. Through three centuries after the Thirty Years War the wars and alliances between these States have been mainly as uninfluenced by religious or Christian considerations as the wars of Græco-Roman history.

Within the several States politics became increasingly secularized. A view prevalent to-day amongst Christians (certainly outside the Roman communion and to some extent within that communion) is that while a right belief about

God and incorporation in the Body of Christ are of supreme importance for each individual, and while the spread of a Christian outlook is of supreme importance for society, it is nevertheless not the province of the State to pronounce on questions of religion; a man's adherence to any of the Christian bodies should be an act of pure individual choice; no privilege or penalty should be attached by the State to membership of any particular religious or anti-religious society. This principle, carried out to the full, means the complete severance of Church and State, the State's complete secularization. In most European countries to-day the principle has been carried out to almost the full extent. It is such a condition of things, and such only, which may be described without qualification as one of religious toleration, or religious freedom. Men associate themselves in co-operation for a great variety of tasks, and the basis of common agreement required differs according to each particular task. The State is an association with the object of securing a number of things which are good from the standpoint of this life, whatever view of the Universe beyond the limits of this life is the true one. A Christian must believe that eternal good is more important than temporal good, but if he believes that temporal goods are also in their measure real goods, he may reasonably co-operate in one political organism, for the purpose of procuring those goods, with men who hold views quite opposed to his own about the Universe. Supposing he co-operated with an atheist in rescuing people from a burning house, that would not prove that he considered it a matter of indifference whether a man did or did not believe in God, but that for the particular work in hand a difference of theological belief was not relevant. Thus many men as keenly interested in theological dogmas as any men have been in the past nevertheless hold that it is good for religion, as well as good for the State, that the State should be confined to the secular sphere, and religion be wholly independent.

When Europe was divided by the Reformation, this separation of Church and State was not seen either on the Catholic or on the Protestant side. It has come about by a gradual process between those days and these. Then, in all States whose rulers were Catholics, the Roman Church continued to have great political power, as it had had in the Middle Ages; but in Protestant States also, the ruling Power was identified with some variety of Reformed religion and gave that religion a position of privilege in the country concerned. Amongst Protestants this association of Church and State was confirmed by the influence of the Old Testament. The Bible was far better known, all parts of it, in Protestant countries (as was natural since Protestantism had made the Bible its exclusive authority and encouraged the reading of it by the people), and since every part was regarded as equally inspired, it is not surprising that the Old

Testament should have seemed to offer a model for the contemporary Christian State. It was especially the Puritan development of Protestantism in England which exhibited a religion of Old Testament type. It assimilated Sunday to the Jewish Sabbath. In Cromwell's shortened Bible for his soldiers prominence was given to the wars in which the children of Israel slaughtered Amalekites and other idolaters: his armies too, he believed, were doing God's work in killing the idolaters of the Anglican Church and destroying the graven images on the façades of their Cathedrals. But even the Church of England was influenced by the Old Testament to the extent of regarding the ancient Israelite king as a model for the King of England. It was the duty of a king of England too to further true religion and suppress aberrations: the nation, as such, should declare its adherence to Anglican Christianity.

Gradually toleration increased. Although the Reformers, as we have seen, had approved of the persecution of heretics, there was, as a matter of fact, much greater liberty after the Reformation in the principal countries of Europe (other than Spain) for the open expression of opinions contrary to the doctrines of the Church. Even in France, where the Roman Church had considerable power and where Protestantism after the Revocation of the Edict of Nantes (in 1685) was crushed or expelled by violent persecution, the great bloom of French literature in the seventeenth and eighteenth centuries was largely secular or sceptical. In England the last burning of a heretic took place under James I. After this, persecution in England only very rarely amounted to actual killing; six Baptists were condemned to death in 1664. Roman Catholics and Protestant Dissenters were subjected to various forms of punishment—fines, confiscation, imprisonment, branding. But in England, as in France, there was considerable liberty in literature. A prominent writer might be a sceptic like Hobbes (1588–1679). There was no restraint under the Stuart kings upon pagan lasciviousness in poetry.

All the time voices were being raised in favour of religious toleration, chiefly among the persecuted Protestant sects. One voice was Milton's. Even in the Anglican Church prominent men (Chillingworth, Jeremy Taylor) pleaded for toleration. Locke, in the last years of the seventeenth century, championed toleration from the side of philosophy. If he excepted Atheists and Roman Catholics, this was because religion in their case seemed to trench upon the political sphere: Atheists, Locke thought, must necessarily be completely unscrupulous in the matter of covenants and oaths, the "bonds of human society," and Roman Catholics were compelled by their religion to be the agents of a "foreign jurisdiction." The Act of Toleration (1689) was a landmark, but though it abolished the penalties formerly inflicted upon Protestant Dissenters, it by no means put them on the same footing as members of the Established Church. It was not till the nineteenth century that complete toleration was established in England—that Roman Catholics, Protestant Dissenters, Jews and Atheists were put on precisely the same footing in regard to the law and given equal political rights. The Houses of Parliament are now no longer specifically Christian bodies, even if the majority of their members may happen to adhere to some form of Christianity.

The process of secularizing the State has not even yet been carried in England to its ultimate possible extension: the Church of England has still some special privileges. The sovereign must by law be an Anglican, and is crowned by Anglican rites. Twenty-six bishops sit in the House of Lords. On the other hand the Church of England has to submit to control by the secularized State: the Prime Minister, who might now be a Jew or an Atheist, designates the person whom, when any see falls vacant, the Dean and Chapter of the Cathedral have, after praying for special guidance by the Holy Spirit, to elect as bishop; and Parliament can forbid an alteration of the liturgy which the Church assemblies have voted. This is obviously an anomalous and transitional state of things. Various considerations hinder the process's being carried to its logical conclusion. One is the fear of a party in the Church that, if the Church were wholly governed by its own ministers, their own party might be in a position of disadvantage. They therefore prefer to see the Church controlled by a secular body, just as one of the women in the judgment of Solomon chose to see the child dead rather than in the possession of the other woman. A way sometimes taken of justifying such an attitude is to say that the Nation and the Church are substantially identical, the Church is only "the Nation on its spiritual side." This might have seemed to be true in days when effective citizenship was limited to Christians, or even to members of the Established Church, but since the secularization of the State has reached the point which it has, it has become a grotesque untruth. It is really a view destructive of the fundamental character of the Christian Church, as a world-wide society to which each person adheres by an individual act of will, not by birth: it assimilates Christianity to the ethnic religions spoken of in the first sentence of this little volume.

From such a perversion as the ethnic view of Christianity the Church of Rome was necessarily free, obviously existing as it did in the form of an organization reaching across all national boundaries with a centre outside any worldly State. Thus in the case of quarrels between kings and their subjects in the seventeenth century the Church of Rome was much more disposed to recognize the rights of peoples against sovereigns than the Church of England: a widely-read book by the Spanish Jesuit Mariana (published in 1599) actually revived the ancient Greek glorification of tyrannicide.

Of course, it was held that both sovereigns and peoples ought to be submissive to the guidance of the Church. While the Roman Church maintained its independence of all worldly governments, it sought to exercise predominant influence upon the governments of countries whose rulers were Roman Catholics. Cardinals and bishops might attain to great personal power, political and social. One main instrument of the Church's power in Spain and in some other countries (the Netherlands, Venice, the Spanish colonies) was the Holy Office, or Inquisition. This organization, deriving its authority from the Pope himself, had been instituted in Spain in 1478. It had power to imprison, try and torture anyone suspected of Judaism or heresy, and those found guilty it handed over to the State to be burnt. It was only of course by concession from the State that an ecclesiastical body like the Inquisition had material force at its command. The horrors now associated with the name of the Inquisition belong chiefly to the fifteenth and sixteenth centuries: in the seventeenth century, even in Spain, the operations of the Inquisition had to become milder, though they were still sufficiently odious. The Liberal and Republican movement which became strong in Europe in the latter part of the eighteenth century was largely anti-clerical and anti-Christian: the Roman Church on its side entered into close alliance with the monarchic Powers. The influence of the Church was widely used in favour of despotism against democracy, just as it was used to suppress the utterance of heretical religious opinions. The Roman Church came to be regarded as the "black" foe of all liberty and intellectual progress. Countries like Spain or Naples or the Papal States offered a picture from which the lovers of freedom and light in Europe recoiled. The opinion has been expressed earlier in this volume that one of the things which chiefly to-day repel men from the Roman Church is the idea (whether true or false) that it gives the priest a commission to interfere unduly in the private concerns of its members. Here we have a second thing, the political record of the Roman Church in the last four centuries. Yet the experience of recent years in Italy and Russia shows that the suppression of free opinion and horrors like those of the Inquisition may go with forms of belief far removed from Catholic Christianity. In former centuries, when the chief European Powers were monarchic, it was with monarchy that Rome allied itself. Now there is no Roman Catholic sovereign left except the King of the Belgians and the King of Italy, with the second of whom the Vatican has only recently come into friendly relations. But there is no essential affinity between Catholicism and monarchy. If in the age to come democracy or communism is in the ascendant, Rome may quite well co-operate with democracy or communism. Already the Roman Church has probably as great a power in the United States as in any European country, and the violent

Republicans in Ireland largely profess to be good Catholics.

If the political record of the Roman Church in the seventeenth and eighteenth centuries weighs heavily against it in the common judgment of men to-day, the political record of the Church of England in those centuries is not exactly glorious.

"No other Church," Lecky wrote, "so uniformly betrayed and trampled on the liberties of her country. In all those fiery trials through which English liberty has passed since the Reformation, she invariably cast her influence into the scale of tyranny, supported and eulogized every attempt to violate the Constitution, and wrote the fearful sentence of eternal condemnation upon the tombs of the martyrs of freedom." [1]

No doubt this rhetoric cannot be taken as a complete statement of the case. It must be remembered that many good men amongst the English clergy were honestly convinced that the injunctions of the New Testament made passive obedience to the sovereign a Christian duty. It did not necessarily mean any contemptible servility of temper. A man of such massive independence of character as Dr. Johnson strongly held this view. The plain meaning of the New Testament text was on that side, though we no doubt to-day consider that directions which St. Paul gave to Christians when they were a small powerless community in the Roman Empire do not apply without qualification to English Christians in the wholly changed conditions of the modern world. It

[1] *The Rise and Influence of Rationalism*, Chapter V

must also be considered that so far as the Puritan assertors of popular liberty sought a Biblical support for their cause, they found it largely in an Old Testament view of the State, which we must pronounce not to be Christian.

It remains to note real difficulties which any attempt to make the separation between Church and State complete must encounter. If the purpose of the State were simply to secure protection for life and property and a general standard of material comfort, the division would be simple enough. But the State regards its functions as extending to care for the mental and moral well-being of all citizens and the observance of certain rules in regard to marriage and the family. But here the State's sphere of concernment overlaps that of the Church, and the problem of adjustment becomes serious.

The two fields upon which collision and conflict between the Church (or the Churches) and the State are always liable to occur are those of education and marriage-law. It lies outside the scope of this small book to examine in what way a *modus vivendi* can best be found in these two fields between the clashing claims. Only in regard to marriage-law a few observations may be made.

If any religious community to which men voluntarily adhere stands for particular principles of conduct in regard to sexual relations, it has a perfect right to insist on all its members conforming to those principles or leaving the community. Any Christian Church is bound to require of its members Christian conduct in these matters, whatever hard renunciations that conduct may demand in individual cases: what precisely Christian conduct is, where opinions about that differ, each community must decide for itself. The problem is: How far ought Christians to try as citizens of a State to make the State Law such that a Christian mode of conduct is enforced upon all subjects of the State alike, though many of them do not adhere to Christianity? Such renunciations as Christianity in certain circumstances demands seem impossible to justify apart from the belief for which Christianity (though not Christianity alone) stands, that man's existence in this world is only a stage in an existence continuing after death, and that it has a probationary or educative purpose in relation to that larger life. A view is sometimes put forward, that belief in a future life is without importance for conduct because to do right without the prospect of a reward hereafter is nobler than to do right with such a prospect. What makes this view nonsensical is that the question, what *is* right, depends in many cases upon the future to be taken into account: the norm of conduct reasonable for an immortal being may be quite unreasonable for the creature of a day. Certain kinds of conduct—for instance, the relief of my neighbour's material needs—may be right, whether there is a future life or not, but in regard to the self-control and renunciation required in sexual relations, the view referred to wholly breaks down. It is no good trying to justify such demands as Christianity on occasion makes—it may be one man's continuing till death under the restrictions of an unsatisfactory marriage, another man's denying the sexual side of his nature any physical fruition—except on the supposition that a man's whole earthly life is only a moment (if a moment of crucial importance) in his personal existence. Have Christians the right, by means of the State Law, to enforce such renunciations upon people who do not believe that there is any life after this ? If you say "No" to this question, you are still confronted with difficulties. For there are grave practical inconveniences where the majority of the population profess Christianity, in having a State Law in regard to marriage different from the law of the Church. Also, if Christians give up the idea of enforcing a Christian norm of conduct upon their non-Christian fellow-citizens, what norm of conduct *are* they, as citizens, to make obligatory by law in these matters for everyone ? It is enough here to indicate that such problems inevitably emerge as the process of secularizing the State goes forward.

In the more or less secularized environment, such as Europe was after the sixteenth century, Christianity had to maintain itself under new and exacting conditions. A great deal that was taken for granted in the Middle Ages had now to be defended against challenge. The change was a tonic for the Christian Church :

it could no longer afford to jog easily along with all the abuses and scandals which had disfigured the times before the Reformation. In the movement called the Counter-Reformation the Roman Church pulled itself together. The Council of Trent (1545–63), regarded by Roman Catholics as Œcumenical, defined Roman doctrines more precisely, and laid down rules for securing a decent state of things in the religious orders. It drew up a Catechism to guide priests in the way the verities of the faith should be set before the laity so as to counteract Protestant perversions. No Popes since the Reformation have repeated the abominations of the Borgias.

Among the agencies by which the Roman Church Militant could carry on its warfare in a world become largely alien or hostile none was more important than the new "Society of Jesus," founded by the Spaniard St. Ignatius Loyola (1491 ?–1556). Jesuits were trained by a severe discipline, not to live in retirement from the world, but to mingle with the world in order to conquer it for the Church. They have played a prominent part in all the subsequent history of the Roman Church and have produced not only religious leaders, but distinguished *savants* in various branches of secular learning. Their world-wide organization, energy and power, have sometimes given them a relative independence, even against other ecclesiastical authorities. They have not always been favourably regarded by bishops, or even by Popes, and with a part of the Roman Catholic laity they are not popular. The Order has been repeatedly expelled from different States, and in 1773 was even temporarily suppressed. Outside the Roman Church two things specially have brought odium upon the name of Jesuit. One is the suspicion of vast subterranean intrigue carried on to gain worldly power (a suspicion which easily attaches to any active world-wide community with an inner life inaccessible to the observation of outsiders—to the Jews, for instance);[1] and the other is the belief that the Jesuits cultivate an immoral casuistry—whence the adjective "jesuitical"—and especially teach that a good end justifies any kind of means. It has often been pointed out that, in the sense supposed, the maxim, The end justifies the means, is really no more Jesuit teaching than it is the teaching of the Church of England or of the Quakers. The *Lettres Provinciales* of the Jansenist Pascal were a witty caricature which has had enormous influence in creating the popular idea of the Jesuits. On the other hand, it is probably true to say that, so far as the Roman Church has used its power to build walls round men's minds over which they must not look, to forbid free inquiry and suppress the utterance of

[1] There are people who see the "hidden hand" of Jesuits everywhere, just as there are other people who see the hidden hand of Jews. Or sometimes it is not even *other* people. The writer has heard of Irish Protestants declaring, "Everybody knows that the Vatican is in the pay of the Jews." (*Sic.*)

heterodox opinion, the Society of Jesus, intent to dominate men for their good, has been the Church's most effective agent. Where it had to deal with a people which was really childlike the result may not have been unhappy: for more than a century and a half (1608–1767) Paraguay under the Jesuit fathers was an immense and delightful nursery, an innocent Paradise shut off from a wicked world.

But it is not only by fresh organization that Christianity has maintained itself during four centuries in a world grown critical. It has continued to produce men and women in whom the distinctively Christian spirit has been powerfully exhibited with a rich variety of individual differences. This has been the case in all the separate communions into which Christendom through the imperfections of human minds has been divided since the sixteenth century. Many Christians whose obedience to what they severally believe to be the declared will of God prevents their joining their separated brethren in the act of communion, nevertheless recognize in Christians outside their own communion the manifestation of the One Spirit. No communion refuses more rigidly than the Roman to join in formal worship with those who are unwilling (if through ignorance) to approach God in the way marked out, Roman Catholics believe, by Christ: yet we find a prominent Roman Catholic writer of to-day explaining that the maxim "Outside the Church no salvation" does not mean that no man can be saved who does not belong to the visible Body governed by the Vicar of Christ.

"The Church," he writes, "is the true and ordinary institute of the grace and truth of Jesus. But that does not prevent there being, alongside this ordinary institute, extraordinary ways of salvation, or hinder the Grace of Christ from visiting particular men without the mediation of the Church. But because and in so far as the Body of Christ comprehends all those who are saved by Christ, those also who are visited by his Grace in this immediate way belong to his Church. It is true that they do not belong to its outward and visible Body, but they certainly belong to its invisible supernatural Soul, to its supernatural 'substance.'"[1]

Any attempt to survey here the persons and movements between the Reformation and the French Revolution wherein the working of the Christian Spirit could be eminently seen is obviously impossible. In the Roman communion we have a new development of ardent Christian mysticism in Spain, whose two chief figures were St. Theresa (1515–82) and St. John (Juan) of the Cross (1542–91); in France, the able and winning shepherd of souls St. Francis of Sales (1567–1622), the great preacher and writer, Bossuet (1627–1704), another great writer on religion, who was also a bishop, Fénelon (1651–1715). In France, again, there was the Jansenist movement, connected with the convent of Port-royal—a movement of strong Puritan character, which resembled Protestantism in laying stress upon Divine Grace, individual conversion, and the reading of the

[1] Karl Adam, *The Spirit of Catholicism*, 1929 (translated from the German, *Das Wesen der Katholizismus*).

Bible amongst the laity, though its doctrine was more exclusive than the authorized Roman one in denying the operation of Grace outside the Roman communion. Jansenism was ultimately condemned by the Pope in the bull *Unigenitus* (1713),[1] but it had produced in the seventeenth century many devoted lives: amongst others, Pascal had adhered to it. Its influence upon the Church at large was great, even where its narrowness was repudiated. In Italy devotion received a notable stimulus through the activity of "the saint of gentleness and kindness," St. Philip Neri (1515–95), who founded the Order of Oratorians, to which Newman attached himself in 1845. St. Theresa, St. John of the Cross, and St. Francis of Sales also perpetuated their work in new religious Orders, as well as in their writings.

When we turn to the countries which followed the Reformed religion we find there, too, devoted and energetic Christian lives. This is one of the things which go to disprove the attempt sometimes made on the Roman side to represent Luther's doctrine of justification by faith as prompted by a desire to get rid of moral restraints and as leading to moral chaos; as a matter of fact, morals showed no relaxation in countries where the predominant religion was Anglican or Protestant, as compared with Roman Catholic countries. No doubt one Protestant country has differed in

[1] The proposition "Grace is not given outside the Church" was, amongst others, declared to be untrue.

this respect from another, as one Roman Catholic country has from another. Curiously, it was precisely that form of Protestantism which went furthest in emphasizing the action of the Divine Will to the exclusion of the human will, Calvinistic Puritanism, which imposed upon society the most rigorous moral code, generating a kind of legalism more gloomy and more onerous than the legalism of the Roman Church, against which the Reformers protested—another case of extremes meeting. The Church of England during those centuries produced its goodly company of saints and Christian writers —George Herbert (1593–1633), parson and poet; John Donne (1573–1631), poet and Dean of St. Paul's; the "judicious Hooker" (1554?–1600), whose book, *The Laws of Ecclesiastical Polity*, is said to have called forth the admiration of Pope Clement VIII; Lancelot Andrewes (1555–1626), Bishop of Winchester; Robert Leighton (1611–84), Archbishop of Glasgow; Jeremy Taylor (1613–67), Bishop of Down and Connor; Thomas Ken (1637–1711), Bishop of Bath and Wells; the philosopher George Berkeley (1685–1753), Bishop of Cloyne; another philosopher, Joseph Butler (1692–1752), Bishop of Durham.

The English Dissenters also made a contribution notable in consideration of their numbers. To Christian poetry they brought the accession of Milton. Two other religious classics came from them, *The Saints' Everlasting Rest* of the Presbyterian, Richard Baxter

(1615–91), and *The Pilgrim's Progress* of the Baptist, John Bunyan (1628–88). We must also reckon here the writings of the early Quakers; those of George Fox himself (1624–91), Robert Barclay (1648–90), John Woolman (1720–72). Perhaps the greatest contribution made by the Dissenters was the continuous testimony they bore, by their very existence, to the character of Christianity as a society to which men adhere by individual conversion and choice, not by birth. The Established Church, just because it formally included all Englishmen who had been christened as babies and did not deliberately leave it, embraced the great multitude of people who had no personal religion at all: it was likely on the other hand that a man belonging to a Dissenting sect belonged to it because that expressed his own personal religious convictions. Inevitably members of the Church of England were always tending to slide into the ethnic view of religion, men belonged to the Church of England simply because they were born Englishmen: Dissenters bore witness to the fact that, if a sect means a particular path [1] which men deliberately choose, Christianity, which had begun as a sect, a *hairesis*, could not cease to be a sect without

[1] Many people have a prejudice against the word "sect" under the impression that it means something "cut off," a schism; but the primary meaning of *secta* in Latin is a *trodden path*: as meaning a sect or philosophic school, it translated the Greek *hairesis*, a "choice," which originally had none of the bad connotation of our "heresy."

ceasing to be Christianity. That was one very great service which Dissenters rendered to the Church.

Since the Renaissance, it was just now said, the intellect of Europe had become in large part critical of Christianity or hostile to it. In the eighteenth century this was more the case than it had ever been since the days of the old Græco-Roman paganism. It has been called the "Age of Rationalism." The richer educated class, "polite society," was pervaded by artificial manners and religious scepticism. Curiously enough, atheism was not at all fashionable, and had few representatives. Most of the prominent men known as "infidels" who during the course of the eighteenth century ridiculed Christianity either believed strongly in a "Supreme Being," as Voltaire and the French Revolutionaries did, or at any rate thought the existence of a Supreme Being probable, though they regarded it as superstitious to believe that the Supreme Being, having once set the Universe going, did anything further in it. Their theory of the Universe is commonly known as Deism.[1] The essence of

[1] Whether the great astronomer, Pierre-Simon Laplace (1749–1827), was really an atheist seems doubtful. The *Catholic Encyclopedia* does not indeed indicate its ground for asserting that Laplace lived and died a Catholic, but it is quite possible that the phrase he used to Napoleon (if the story is true)—that he "saw no need for the theistic hypothesis"—meant no more than that he regarded it as irrelevant to bring in the theistic hypothesis when you were giving a scientific explanation of the movements of the heavenly bodies, a thing which a Christian might quite well say.

the eighteenth-century Rationalism was the disposition to believe that this was a plain, easily intelligible world, clear and regular and without mystery, like the buildings and the formal gardens of that age. Just as morals were simple, because you had only to take the "common-sense" rules of decency recognized by European society in the eighteenth century as laws of reason universally valid for the human race, so human history was simple if you explained everything by the "common-sense" generalizations got by observing the everyday conduct of contemporary men. To such a view Christianity was, of course, repugnant. Christianity implied that something wholly new had broken in at a particular moment of history, which those common-sense generalizations could not explain; it purported to set before the mind a Reality which transcended satisfactory formulation by human thoughts working on the basis of human experience. It implied even that there were fields of human experience outside the circle lit up by lucid syllogistic common sense. All this made Christianity an offence and an absurdity in the formal eighteenth-century world.

Any religion which becomes the religion of the majority and turns into habit tends to grow humdrum and flat, in whatever flame of enthusiasm it may have originated. It is only by new movements making here and there new starts that life in a church can be revived, which new movements often themselves with time become dead habit. At the beginning of the eighteenth century life in the Church of England was low: religion had lost all hold upon a great part of the manual workers, whose lives were sordid and brutal. It was the Methodist movement connected with the names of John Wesley (1703–91) and George Whitefield (1714–70) which made the immense difference. The movement arose within the Anglican Church; the first "Methodists" were a group of young High-Churchmen at Oxford who tried to live by a severe rule. But the impulse which made Wesley an Evangelist came from German Protestants, Moravian missionaries. Through contact with them Wesley went through an experience which turned him from the painful observance of rules to the assurance of having been saved by Divine Grace and the urgent desire to bring the same salvation to the godless masses in England. The open-air preaching of Wesley and his associates had a wonderful effect. Though the clergy of the Anglican Church largely opposed the movement as something novel and tainted with "enthusiasm,"[1] Wesley himself remained an Anglican to the last. His followers, with his reluctant sanction, formed the Wesleyan community separate from the Anglican Church. The whole religious life of England far outside the limits of that community was affected by

[1] It is of course unfair to represent utterances of eighteenth-century divines against "enthusiasm," as being directed against what *we* call enthusiasm. The word then had a different meaning: it meant what we call "fanaticism" to-day.

the Movement. The Evangelical Movement, both within and without the Church of England, was one outcome of it.

Like the Reformed religion in England, Protestantism in Germany also in the seventeenth and eighteenth centuries largely became a dead habit. There, too, life was revived by the set of people called Pietists. The best memorial they have left of themselves is the great number of hymns, simple and ardent, in which German Protestantism is much richer than English, although Methodism made a change here, for John Wesley's brother Charles was a genuine poet, the author of many of the hymns most commonly sung to-day in churches.

It is probably in the hymns of German Protestants such as Paul Gerhardt (1607–76) and Gerhardt Tersteegen (1697–1769) and in the English Methodist hymns, that the heart of old Protestant devotion is best revealed. And what is striking is how little Christian devotion differs here in its central burning point from the most central utterances of Roman Catholic devotion. If these Protestants have rejected a great part of the Catholic tradition, what they retain is sufficiently remarkable. No one could regard this as anything of the nature of a cold and abstract Theism. Like the most central Catholic devotion, it is devotion directed to the vividly apprehended Person of Jesus, apprehended not as a mere human figure which might be the object of a sentimental affection, but as one who is God come down in the infinite condescension of love, and love for whom is fused with the awe and worship belonging to God. Very great theological differences divide the author of

> Jesu, dulcedo cordium,
> Fons vitæ, lumen mentium,
> Excedis omne gaudium
> Et omne desiderium,[1]

from the author of

> Jedes Herz will etwas lieben;
> Liebt's nicht Jesum, kann's nicht ruh'n:
> Mein Herz, Herr, ist dir verschrieben;
> Zu Dir will's, so nimm es nun.
> Lass mich alle Welt verhöhnen,
> Jesus soll mein Liebster sein:
> Schönste unter allen Schönen,
> Du gefällst mir nur allein,[2]—(G. TERSTEEGEN.)

and the author of

> Jesu, Lover of my soul,
> Let me to thy bosom fly—(CHARLES WESLEY.)

but how enormously more important than the things which divide them is the astounding belief in which, as against everything outside Christianity, they are one!

Some of these Protestants may have thought it wrong to use a material crucifix in order to set before their eyes the supreme self-sacrifice.

[1] St. Bernard. It is the hymn which in our familiar English version begins "Jesu, thou joy of loving hearts, Thou fount of life, thou light of men."

[2] "Every heart must love something; unless it love Jesus, it cannot rest. My heart, Lord, is all given to Thee; it yearneth after Thee; O take it then. Let me contemn all the world; Jesus shall be my Most Beloved, fairest among all the fair: I have joy in Thee alone."

But they would use all the resources of language to create in the mind a visual image exactly corresponding.

Setze dich, mein Geist, ein wenig ;
  Und beschau' dies Wunder gross,
Wie dein Gott und Ehrenkönig
  Hängt am Kreuze nackt und bloss.
Schau die Liebe, die ihn triebe
Zur dir aus des Vaters Schoos.[1]—(G. TERSTEEGEN.)

When I survey the wondrous cross,
  Where the young Prince of glory died . . .
See, from his head, his hands, his feet,
  Sorrow and love flow mingled down . . .—(I. WATTS.)

And if the reaction to such an image in the worshipper was a new resolution to devote his whole person to the great Lover and to the utmost service of the men for whom he died—a service in which self-righteousness would be kept off by the thought of the tremendous debt which could never be paid—was there much to distinguish that from the state of mind with which a Roman Catholic rose from his knees before the crucifix or before the Blessed Sacrament on an occasion when his offering of prayer had been touched by the fire from heaven? That was the old Protestantism, the Protestantism which had rejected so much of Catholicism, but which still held fast to the old Catholic creeds and the substantial part of the old Catholic Bible.

[1] "Sit thee down a little, my soul, and contemplate this great wonder, how thy God and King hangs upon the cross bare and naked. Look on the love which drove him, out from the bosom of the Father, to thee."

CHAPTER X

FROM THE FRENCH REVOLUTION TO THE PRESENT DAY

After the picture of a neatly rational, fairly stable world which had possessed the minds of European men in the eighteenth century had been rudely disturbed by the French Revolution and the Napoleonic convulsions, the general outlook on the Universe underwent a notable change. The end of the eighteenth, and beginning of the nineteenth, century was marked by what we know as the Romantic Movement. The characteristic of the movement is that it diverted interest from self-satisfied rationalism, with its limited intellectual clarity, to vaguer, more loosely ranging sentiment and imagination, to instincts that seemed to lie deeper than reason, to obscure suggestions that seemed to bring the soul into contact with a reality rich and wonderful, though impossible to comprehend and define. The ideal world to which men turned was no longer an imaginary classical world of clearly-marked regular patterns, but an imaginary Middle Ages with dim-lit cathedrals and haunted forests, with confused picturesqueness and strange adventures, or an imaginary still older primitive world, which was found revealed in the spurious poems of Ossian. The world of imagination had no hard frontiers marking it off from unexplored immensity. The eighteenth century had believed in rational norms for life and art, stereotyped for the whole human species: the Romantic Movement created a fresh interest in the peculiar varieties of different traditions; it helped to accentuate Nationalism against Cosmopolitanism, historical perspective against flat uniform generalization.

As the nineteenth century went on, two other great interests came to occupy the minds of Europeans, in one way stemming the Romantic Movement, and in another way entering into combination with it. One was the interest in Natural Science. The century saw an advance in experimental science such as no period in the history of mankind before could show. The scientific devices which, one after another, came to furnish the life of ordinary men, devices which enabled them to have their bodies transported through space at a speed never approached before, or communicate with each other in words over vast distances, or destroy each other in war on a gigantic scale, could not fail to impress men deeply with belief in Science as the one trustworthy guide to life. The scientific faith was substantiated by its works. The Scientific Movement in this way came as a corrective and tonic to the vague range of sentiment and imagination which the Romantic Movement had brought about. But in the study of history and anthropology the scientific temper and the romantic to some extent worked together: both were concerned to seize the specific varieties in the manifold expressions of the spirit of man. The historical work of the nineteenth century and of our own, with its imaginative reconstruction of the past, is an outcome of the Romantic Movement and the Scientific Movement together.

In so far as the new rationalism was opposed to the Romantic Movement it checked it, but never suppressed it. All through the nineteenth century there ran an anti-intellectualist strain: many minds held fast to the conviction that instinct or sentiment or practical value gave men a truer apprehension of reality than reason logical and scientific. Again and again in the great writers of the century, especially in the poets, this conviction found utterance. As a reaction against scientific rationalism, it gained even fresh strength in our own generation, issuing in such philosophies as that of Bergson or the Pragmatism of F. C. S. Schiller and William James.

The third great interest which supervened in the nineteenth century was that of social and economic reconstruction. Side by side with the great scientific development went an industrial development no less astounding: this increased prodigiously the material wealth of mankind, but was accompanied by dark evils in the life of the workers, massed together on an ever-increasing scale in the enormous factories which rose in hundreds of European cities. The spectacle of these evils, from the early years of the nineteenth century, turned the minds of some thinkers to speculations regarding a radical change in the arrangements of society, by which the wealth, now distributed with such glaring inequality, would be distributed equally, the distinction of classes abolished, and a life relatively easy and interesting made possible for everybody. Such speculations gave rise to all the various forms of Socialism put forward in the last hundred years, and speculative Socialism was accompanied by the Labour Movement in the different civilized countries, which by practical agitation secured, wherever it could, an amelioration in detail of the lot of the manual worker. This is not the place to discuss how far any of the Socialist schemes put forward are capable of removing present ills without creating greater ones: it is enough to note that the present ills have caused profound disquiet to the minds of many good men, and that the desire to bring about a better constitution of society is a dominant interest of the present day. This is true, even though in many respects the lot of the manual worker to-day is far better than it was two or three generations ago.

These three movements—the Romantic Movement, the Scientific Movement and the Socialist Movement—have made the environment in which the Christianity of the last three or four generations has lived. To trace its reactions to them is to trace a great part of its inner life.

In so far as eighteenth-century Voltairian rationalism had been antagonistic to Christianity, the Romantic Movement was favourable to it. In his *Génie du Christianisme* and in his romance entitled *Les Martyrs*, Chateaubriand (1768–1848), the chief representative of the Romantic Movement in France, came forward with a defence of Christianity on Romantic lines. It was, of course, Christianity in its Roman Catholic form which Chateaubriand exalted. With all its wealth of ancient visible symbols and emotional suggestion it could be exhibited as satisfying the sentimental and imaginative nature of men far better than the old jejune rationalism. Although in its day Chateaubriand's splendid rhetoric gave his work immense influence in shaping the thoughts and feelings of the new Europe, it may seem to us now to have little substance behind it. We care less than the world did then for mere eloquence, and the Roman Church to-day would certainly not rest its case on such a defence. Chateaubriand's own life was hardly that of a saint, and his interest in religion was in some measure literary rather than personal.

In German Protestantism the Romantic Movement expressed itself in another way. The outstanding figure in German Protestant theology in the early part of the nineteenth century was Schleiermacher (1768–1834). His philosophy of religion showed the new tendency to give value in religion to feeling rather than intellectual theory: Schleiermacher taught that the very basis of religion was a sense of dependence on the Unseen Power. The Kantian philosophy, then dominant in Germany, might serve to strengthen an anti-intellectualist interpretation of Christianity; for Kant, after having in his *Critique of Pure Reason* disparaged the Understanding as a means of apprehending reality, had based conduct upon faith in God and in the immortality of the Soul, demanded, he held, by the *practical* Reason. The theology of Albrecht Ritschl (1822–89), which exerted so widespread an influence through all the latter part of the nineteenth century, not only in Germany, was framed directly under the influence of Kant, and showed the anti-intellectualist tendency in a new form. Ritschlianism regarded all metaphysics—that is to say, all attempts to coordinate beliefs about the unseen world with rational knowledge of the visible world in a coherent system of thought—as an unwholesome admixture in Christianity. The essence of Christianity was the impression made upon men directly by the historical Jesus, an impression which produced a confidence in God's goodwill, an experience of inner liberation. No religion got by the working of men's minds, got in any way except through the Person of Jesus, was the real thing: but you must equally dismiss all beliefs about the Person of Jesus which had to do with his real relation to God, his preexistence or his personal activity after his death. All that was metaphysics: you must not try to rationalize the impression made by the Figure in the Gospels, but you must rest content with your immediate experience of the impression. One may see in Ritschlianism an attempt to combine an affective temper derived from old-fashioned Lutheran piety with a philosophic scepticism which might save piety from coming into collision with the results of rational inquiry.

Christianity in England during the earlier part of the nineteenth century was not yet much affected by any of the three movements which have been described. The most living element in English religion at that time was still the Evangelicalism which carried on the Methodist Movement of the eighteenth century. The "Oxford Movement," on the other hand, in the middle of the nineteenth century did show a special form of the tendency which the Romantic Movement had initiated. It had affinities with the Romantic Movement, not so much in its anti-intellectualist character as in its direction of interest to Medieval Catholicism. Yet the anti-intellectual tendency of the Romantic Movement appeared in the teaching of Newman, the philosopher of the Oxford Movement. His *Grammar of Assent*, published after he had joined the Roman Church, was an important contribution: in this he found the basis of belief in an "illative sense," something more direct than the conclusion of a process of reasoning which could be set out in words.

No Christian body as a whole committed itself to the anti-intellectualist position, but individual teachers have inclined to it. At the time, for instance, when Pragmatism was in vogue, the late J.N. Figgis put forward a defence of Christianity on similar anti-intellectualist lines in his book *The Gospel and Human Needs* (2nd Edition, 1912). An analogous defence of Catholic Christian practice was put forward by the Roman Catholic Modernists, notably by E. Le Roy, and by George Tyrrell in his *Lex Orandi* (1903) and *Lex Credendi* (1906) But the Roman Church, with its strong tradition of Scholastic intellectualism, could not possibly accept a Pragmatic construction of Christianity, such as that put forward by some of the Modernists.

The second of the determining movements of the nineteenth century was the Scientific Movement. In contact with this, traditional beliefs in the Christian Churches underwent searching revision, and even Roman Catholic Christianity has come out of the ordeal with some modifications (though Roman Catholics would of course maintain that the essentials of the faith remain unchanged).

The Christian tradition did not indeed conflict with Natural Science, in the narrower sense of that term, except in regard to the origins of the world and of the human race. A great shock to traditional belief came from the Darwinian theory of the origin of the human species published to the world in 1859. Even apart from its assertion that man had been developed by a gradual process from the lowest forms of animal life—the chief offence—its putting back the date when man first appeared upon the globe to an incalculable number of thousands of years ago upset the whole traditional view of the place taken by the history of Israel and of the Christian Church in the total scheme of man's past. The Darwinian view also seemed to be incompatible with the belief that a Fall had taken place at any moment in the past, when man had passed from a state of blissful innocence in a Paradise to a state of hereditary sinfulness, and the belief in a Fall seemed essential to the Christian doctrine of redemption. It is no wonder that Darwinism was at first denounced by every section of the Christian community as a deadly error. Within the seventy-three years which have elapsed since 1859, the great bulk of educated Christians have accepted the truth of Darwinism so far as to believe that the body and intellectual faculties of man came into being as the term of a process of physical descent from lower animal forms extending over the thousands of years which Science demands. The number of educated Christians in England who would now deny this is a negligible quantity : they form only a small section in the Evangelical party without any standing in the community at large. It is only the extreme ignorance of journalists and a large proportion of the public, regarding what is taught in the churches, which makes it possible for any churchman to-day to acquire prestige, as daring and modern, by publicly asserting his belief in Evolution ; he is merely asserting what for some time past has been a commonplace of theological schools. On the other hand, Christians generally would deny that the development of man could be completely accounted for by the action of physical laws working casually without any Divine Purpose; they would not hold that Darwinism gives a complete explanation. And in regard to this apparently a number of men of science with no theological bias would now agree with them.

The acceptance of Darwinism to the extent indicated has greatly modified the Christian outlook on the world. Yet modern Christians would contend that there is no conflict between Darwinism, so understood, and the essential Christian belief that man has come into being by Divine Power in order to realize a Divine Purpose and that a supernatural life entered humanity with the creation of the Church. How the harmony between the Christian faith and the new belief about the origins of man is presented by different Christian thinkers of our time, the limits of this little volume do not allow of our examining. There are naturally differences between one Christian thinker's construction and another's, just as there are between one non-Christian thinker's and another's. It is only by going direct to the published writings of each of them that anyone can form a fair judgment regarding the validity of his particular construction.

It is sometimes supposed that the question of miracles was the one regarding which the conflict between traditional belief and Natural

Science was the most acute. But this is a popular delusion. The belief in miracles does not conflict with any of the Natural Sciences: what it conflicts with is a particular philosophical theory, held indeed by many men of science, but not itself demonstrated, or even demonstrable, by any scientific method. A biologist cannot, as such, pronounce that the story of a man being raised from the dead is untrue. All that a biologist, as a biologist, can say is that the raising of a man from the dead implies the coming into operation of a force of which, in the whole field investigated by Biology, no trace has been found. To which the believer in miracles can answer: "Of course no trace has been found, because the force in question *ex hypothesi* comes into operation in this way only on very rare occasions, perhaps many centuries apart." If to this the biologist replies: "I do not believe that such a force exists in the Universe," he is speaking, no longer as a biologist, but as a philosopher. And a man may be a very good biologist and a very poor philosopher.

While, however, the conflict between Natural Science and traditional belief came about solely in regard to the origins of the world and of man, very much graver difficulties arose from the undermining of important parts of traditional belief by Anthropology. Anthropology may be called a Science in one sense: it involves the systematic examination and classification of facts and the valuation of human testimony on certain fixed principles. But since it deals with the behaviour of men, it deals with something which is not measurable and calculable as merely material processes are: Anthropology is a Science only in the way that History is a Science: indeed their two fields overlap.

Yet an inference, even if only a probable one, may be one of a very high degree of probability, if based on a large knowledge of the facts. The facts regarding the behaviour of men, especially in regard to religion, at the lower levels of culture, and in the various civilizations, past and present, all over the globe, became generally known, thanks to the anthropological research of the nineteenth century, as they had never been known before. This set the Christian religion in a larger context of human religion generally and many constituents in it took on a new appearance in consequence. The resemblances discovered between Christianity and other religions in themselves made it difficult for some inquirers to believe in Christianity's claim to be the one religion for mankind—and Christianity is either this or it is altogether nonsense. It is *here* that the difficulty of miracles came in. No philosophy and no natural science could prove miracles to be impossible, but Anthropology showed the belief in miracles to be common all the world over, wherever there was not a high level of rational culture, and it was usually admitted that the belief in miracles was everywhere, outside the sacred Jewish and Christian history, a delusion. It is therefore a wrong figure to speak of the belief in miracles conflicting with established fact: it is not a case of conflict, but of a weakening of the reasons which impel men to believe.

Examination of the writings produced by men of different civilizations and at different times, with a view to discovering how they were constructed, distinguishing the authors where the work is composite, ascertaining the ideas and modes of behaviour which they reflect, and the degree to which they give an accurate account of real events—all this is a part of Anthropology in the large sense of the term. And the gravest shock of all sustained by traditional belief in the nineteenth century came from anthropological inquiry of this sort—what was called the "Higher Criticism" of the Scriptures. This meant a minute examination of the collection of writings of various dates bound up together in the Bible with a view to analysing their constituents and determining their character, as historical documents, on the same principles as those applied in the examination of other human literatures. The result of the inquiry was to make it probable (with a degree of probability in some cases approaching certainty) that the process by which they had come about was often quite different from that supposed by traditional belief. Some of the writings were recognized to be documents contemporary with the events they recorded, of high historical value; others appeared to be fiction, whose statements were widely at variance with ascertained historical fact, sometimes with each other;

some writings which had been supposed to be the work of a single author showed every appearance of having come together bit by bit, through the combinations and additions of different scribes over long periods of time. The Bible came out of the ordeal as a collection of writings of a very high order, from the literary, from the historical, and from the religious, point of view, but a collection which contained also a considerable amount of human error. It was all up with the infallibility of Scripture, if the conclusions of the critics were true.[1]

This was the worst of the waves which broke upon Christianity in the nineteenth century from the scientific side. The Roman Church maintained its doctrine of the Divine inspiration of all the writings included in the Roman canon with no great change, though its interpretation of the infallibility of Scripture is in some respects not as rigid as the doctrine of verbal inspiration in old-fashioned Protestantism. Exactly how far a Roman scholar may go in admitting modern critical theories is uncertain. The Modernists went as far as any scholars, except the most extreme, in other Christian communities have gone, but the Modernists were sternly suppressed

[1] No doubt the opposition to critical views of the Bible was largely strengthened by the popular misunderstanding of the term "critic." As used by the critics it meant simply what *kritikos* meant in Greek, a literary expert; but since to "criticize" in English commonly means "to find fault," it was generally supposed that the main object of the critical school was to pick holes in the Bible and disparage its value.

by Pius X; the most eminent Biblical critic in their group, the French priest, Alfred Loisy, not only severed his connexion with the Roman Church, but also abandoned Christianity. What, however, makes it uncertain where Rome will finally draw the line is that the public teaching of a particular view may be forbidden by the Roman authorities as dangerous, without Rome committing itself to the assertion that the view is untrue, or making it impossible for the view to be put forward with ecclesiastical permission later on.[1]

The Roman Church is in a position to maintain the Divine authority of the writings included in the particular collection which constitutes the Catholic Canon with greater logical consistency than Protestants, because Roman Catholics consider the judgment of the Church determining which books are Divinely inspired to be infallible, and their belief in the inspiration of

[1] It is common knowledge amongst scholars that the verse which appears in our Authorized Version as 1 John, v. 7 (speaking of the Trinity as the "three who bear witness in heaven"), not found in any old Greek manuscript, was inserted in the Latin Bible in the fourth century, probably in Spain. In 1897 the Holy Office in Rome, the highest ecclesiastical tribunal, made an authoritative pronouncement, approved and confirmed by Leo XIII, that it was not safe to deny that this verse was an authentic part of St. John's epistle. But in 1905 Professor Künstle, a Roman Catholic priest, was allowed to issue a dissertation on this verse, with the *imprimatur* of the Archbishop of Freiburg, in which he set out to demonstrate that the verse was composed in Spain in 390 by the heretic Priscillian.

the Scriptures is thus an organic part of a whole system of belief.

It is common to represent those Evangelicals who stood for the verbal infallibility of the Bible without compromise as stupidly obscurantist. This is unfair. It should be recognized that they had a true sense, when they felt that the slightest admission of the possibility of error in any statement of Scripture meant the admission of a principle which might corrode the whole basis upon which the old Protestantism stood. The change of view in some "moderate" critical theory might not affect anything central for the faith—the question, for instance, whether the later chapters of Isaiah were by Isaiah himself or by a somewhat later prophet (who may, for all we know, have been called Isaiah too); but once allow that the constituents of a book of Scripture can be determined by considerations of probability according to the natural working of the human mind, and you cannot stop the application of the same principles of inquiry to parts of the Bible which concern the Christian faith far more nearly—to the four Gospels, for instance. When some "moderate" critic invited them to accept the "new light thrown on the Bible," as something which would make no difference to their faith, they rightly saw that they were being asked to desert what seemed solid ground for a sea of doubtful questions. The event has proved that the defenders of verbal infallibility were justified in their fears. For now that belief in the infallibility of Scripture has been given up by the great mass of Protestant Christianity, the old Protestantism is rapidly withering away like a flower severed from its root. Inevitably Protestantism to-day is sliding into Unitarianism: those communities outside the Roman and Orthodox Churches which still maintain the old Gospel are the communities which retain a certain regard for tradition, for the authority which a belief derives from the fact that it has actually been a belief underlying the specifically Christian life throughout the centuries, apart from its statement in a text of Scripture. A Protestantism which has lost the old anchorage, belief in the infallibility of Scripture, can save itself from the drift to Unitarianism only by returning in some way to belief in the value of Christian tradition. Such belief is probably an essential element in the new movement in German Protestantism initiated by Karl Barth, which was said to have won large numbers of the younger men. For while Barthianism represents in some respects a violent recoil from the Liberalism of the last generation and a return to an old Evangelical idea of salvation, it leaves the field free for the most radical theories regarding the books of the Bible. One might feel a greater confidence in the future of this movement if it did not seem at present to operate so much with defiant paradoxical assertion; but as an attempt to divert the current of Protestantism in another direction, away from Unitarian Liberalism, the movement is of profound interest, and from the issue of the attempt, whatever it may be, the Church is likely to gain valuable instruction. Will it be possible to find a durable form of Protestantism without a larger return to tradition than even the Barthians are yet willing to make?

If, however, the nineteenth-century Protestant defenders of the doctrine of verbal infallibility were so far right, their position was nevertheless untenable. This explains why the number of old Evangelicals who alone to-day in the British Isles adhere to this doctrine have shrunk to a small group without influence among the educated, a group which goes on shrinking as death removes one after another of its veterans. The position is untenable because it involves a self-contradiction. The fundamental dogma of this type of Protestantism is that no doctrine or practice is to be accepted as belonging to the Christian faith unless it is stated in a particular collection of ancient writings. But this fundamental dogma is itself nowhere found in those writings. The New Testament knows nothing of the New Testament: no writing included in the New Testament gives any hint of its belonging to a particular collection, or of the fact that a collection of Christian writings is going to be made which will constitute a body of canonical scriptures. Much less is there any statement in the New Testament to declare which writings will be included. None of the four Gospels ascribes authority to any of the other three, or claims infallible inspiration for itself: St. Luke even begins by inviting confidence on the ground that he has made special investigations, precisely as a secular historian might do. The belief that the writings included in the New Testament are of peculiar Divine authority is derived simply from a judgment of the Church, gradually solidified, as we have seen, in the first seven or eight centuries, a judgment of that very Church which Protestantism affirms to have fallen in other respects grievously into error and to have made a mistake in regard to the books of the Old Testament.

It is, of course, true that, quite apart from any formal judgment of the Church regarding the value of the books of the New Testament, these writings are documents of the first Christian generations and show what Christianity was like near its source. As such they may well be taken by Christians of subsequent ages as classical and normative for the Christian life. So far as the epistles of St. Paul in the New Testament are genuine utterances of the Apostle (it is only in regard to 2 Thessalonians, Ephesians, and the Pastoral Epistles that doubt is entertained by any body of opinion that counts, and the authenticity of the two first is maintained to-day by many first-class scholars) Christians may with good reason ascribe to them a quite peculiar authority. Yet, apart from a judgment of the Church, there is no ground for treating every statement in them as an infallible utterance of God. Or again, Christians must always recur to the words of the Lord, and, quite apart from the judgment of the Church, anyone with literary sense, who is not merely a crank or a philological pedant, must feel that the utterances of Jesus in our Synoptic Gospels have too strong an individuality not to be in the main the utterances of one real Man. Yet, in the case of our earliest Gospel, what we have is only what St. Mark recollected of what St. Peter recollected of what Jesus had said some thirty-eight years before Peter's death, and that translated from Aramaic into Greek, so that it is absurd, apart from the Church's judgment, to press every clause or every sentence in the words attributed to Jesus, as if they had been taken down at the time by a phonograph or by shorthand.

There was one matter beside Biblical Criticism in regard to which the "Broad" school, within and without the Church of England, initiated a general change of belief amongst Christians—the doctrine of everlasting punishment. Belief in this had been generally professed by Christians from the early centuries of the Christian era up to the nineteenth century. When teachers of the "Broad" school first denounced as abominable the belief that the greater part of mankind, or indeed any part of mankind, was destined to undergo torment for ever and ever, they had against them not only the Roman Church, for which eternal punishment was a dogma defined irrevocably, but the bulk of the Church of England and Protestant Nonconformity. To-day only a small section of the Evangelicals continue to believe that all who die unconverted, including the whole of the non-Christian world, except children who die before they reach the age of moral responsibility, will endure anguish in hell for ever. The few people left who hold this belief find some consolation in thinking of the vast infant mortality in countries outside Europe. Such Evangelicals are happier than St. Augustine in so far as they do not think the baptism of babies a necessary condition of their salvation. The Roman Church is committed to the doctrine of the eternal punishment of those who die impenitent in mortal sin. Yet few educated Roman Catholics now hold the doctrine of eternal punishment in the same sense in which it was held by Dante, or indeed by Roman Catholics generally before the nineteenth century. It may here be noted that modern views of the fate of those who die unsaved re-interpret or repudiate either the adjective or the substantive in the phrase "eternal punishment." Some, that is to say, teach that the punishment involves real pain, but that it is not for ever, others that the punishment is really for ever, but that it is not torment as pictured in the old view. The latter is the line taken by present-day Roman Catholics and some, no doubt, in other Christian bodies. It was strongly urged by the late Baron Friedrich von Hügel, whose influence is so wide outside his own communion. He argued that the punishment must be everlasting, in so far as no view could be right which made it come to the same thing in the end whether a person did or did not obey the Divine call in this life of probation. Those who refused the supernatural call here would never be able to attain what they might have attained, if they had made the right choice; and the abiding loss would involve some kind of pain. But it is established Roman doctrine that the good remaining to the lost outbalances the pain, so that continued existence is for them preferable to annihilation. No Catholic is bound by a dogma of the Church to believe that the number of the damned exceeds the number of the saved. Some teachers of the Roman Communion (so the writer of this little book has been assured) even explain that although it is *de fide* to believe that any man, if he directs his will up to his death in a certain way, incurs eternal punishment, it is permissible to hope that no man ever actually has directed his will, or has continued to direct his will, in that particular way. This opinion of course, if it is really held, is a purely private one, not as yet authorized by the Church. With regard to babies dying unbaptized, the Roman doctrine is that, while they cannot attain to the Divine Vision which is man's full felicity, they have eternal existence in a "Limbo"—a "Borderland" whose conditions are much preferable to those of earthly life. This seems hardly to differ from the Pelagian doctrine, which allowed them to attain eternal life, but not the Kingdom of God, except that Catholics would not give the name "eternal life" to existence in the Limbo.

On the other hand it was the adjective "eternal" upon which many fastened. The Greek adjective *aionios*, it was alleged, connected with punishment in the New Testament, does not mean "everlasting," but "lasting for a very long time" or "belonging to the other world." This contention, though it afforded many people a way of relief from the doctrine of everlasting punishment, is hardly sound as a matter of linguistics. It went upon the common fallacy that you can determine the meaning of a word from its derivation, which is often not the case: when the New Testament was written *aionios* did ordinarily mean "everlasting." The view that the punishment of the lost will ultimately come to an end was adopted in two different forms. According to one, punishment ends in the annihilation of the sinful soul: its sin is in fact gradually destructive of its being, so that sooner or later it ceases to exist. This form of belief was the one adopted by a large number of Evangelicals, and is probably the one prevalent to-day in the Evangelical party except for the small section which still adheres to the doctrine of everlasting torment. Men of the "Broad" school usually have adopted the other form of belief, that the punishment ends by the sinful soul being purified, so that it attains the condition of bliss. Hell, in the phrase which Browning puts into the mouth of a Pope, is the state

> "Where God unmakes but to re-make the soul
> He else made first in vain; which must not be."

The writer of this little volume has heard one of the most highly-placed and deservedly respected teachers in the Church of England declare it as his belief that sins would be so turned by repentance hereafter to spiritual profit that at long last the worst sinner would be glad to have had every bit of experience which he had had. This view contrasts markedly with the Roman view, even in the form in which it was presented by Baron von Hügel, though it has a certain affinity to what Dante says about the attitude of the redeemed in heaven to the sins of their earthly life: "Here there is no repentance any more: there is only laughter—not at the wickedness, for that comes to mind no longer, but because of the Divine Goodness which ordered everything to the end it had in view" (*Paradiso*, IX, 103–5). *Felix culpa!* Undoubtedly the doctrine has its dangers in application.

The third signal movement which we noticed in the nineteenth century was the Labour Movement. By this too Christianity has been profoundly affected. It must be remembered that Socialism on the Continent, unlike English Socialism, has been, as a whole, bitterly anti-Christian.[1] The almost inevitable consequence has been that Continental Catholicism is anti-Socialist. Yet many Roman Catholics have felt that the existing arrangements of society did

[1] The writer remembers having read in a German paper the account of a Protestant pastor who had joined the Social-Democrat party, but got into great trouble with the party simply because in some public speech he had referred to Jesus as "der Heiland (the Saviour)." This gives a measure of the intolerance prevailing in those circles.

involve evils with which the Christian Church was bound to concern itself, and have identified themselves with the cause of the manual workers who seek better conditions of life. Movements for democratic social reform on Catholic lines have not been wanting. It will be remembered how closely in England Cardinal Manning was associated with such a movement. In Germany the important *Christliche Gewerkvereine* (Christian Trade Unions) numbering many thousands of adherents amongst the manual workers, were mainly Catholic and under ecclesiastical direction. (The Catholic *Volksverein* for men were given in Elster's *Handwörterbuch für Staatswissenschaften* (1926) as having about 700,000 members, the *Katholische Frauenbund* for women as having 250,000 members.) An important event in this connexion was the pronouncement of Pope Leo XIII in his Encyclical *Rerum Novarum* (May 15, 1891). This pronouncement has been supplemented by another of Pope Pius XI, *Quadragesimo anno*, delivered on May 15, 1931. The aim of these pronouncements is to put again before the world the idea of an ordered Christian society as set forth by St. Thomas Aquinas, with modifications adapting it to the present state of the world. On the one hand some of the presuppositions of the Socialist theory are repudiated, on the other hand Capitalism, so far as it means selfish individualism, is condemned. Socialists, of course, will none of these counsels.

In England, when the Evangelical movement

was strong at the beginning of the nineteenth century, there could be no attempt to amalgamate Christianity and Socialism. Evangelicals held perfectly logically that it was more important for a man to be converted and secure a happy eternity than to have his circumstances made more comfortable for a few years here and then pass to eternal misery. Amongst Evangelicals too the old expectation of a proximate Return of the Lord was common: it would not be worth while to attempt a thorough re-casting of earthly institutions. Yet it should be fairly recognized that Evangelicals showed conspicuous zeal in getting some of the particular evils attaching to society, as it was, remedied. It was Evangelicals who by patient and strenuous efforts obtained the freeing of all negro slaves in the British dominions and the abolition of the slave-trade (1807). It was the Evangelical Lord Shaftesbury (1801–85) who obtained the suppression of child-labour in factories and other reforms, and who interested himself actively in such things as Ragged Schools and the housing of the poor. At the present day the Salvation Army, an Evangelical body, carries on an important work of social service and reclamation beside its evangelistic activities. But it was the leaders of the Broad Church party, especially F. D. Maurice (1805–72) and Charles Kingsley (1819–75), who first put before the British public the ideals of Christian Socialism. It soon became a common belief that the Church had made a mistake in directing its interest so predominantly to the other world, that it was an essential part of its business to "build Jerusalem" in this world. Plainly a swing in this direction was liable to go too far and divert the Christian Church from its true mission; it also naturally led to some well-meaning clergymen taking a passionate part in economic controversies for which they had no special illumination. While Christianity lays it down that a man should devote himself to securing his neighbour's good to the utmost of his ability, it does not tell him in detail what the best means for securing his neighbour's good are, but leaves that to be determined by earthly experience and reason. Yet Christian Socialism has one great truth behind it. Christians cannot show that their concern for men's eternal good is based on real love for men unless they show also concern for men's temporal good. Also some of the bad material conditions in the lives of the poor are actually a great hindrance to their getting spiritual good. The early Christian Church, which felt that it expressed the spirit of its Lord by making him say to the multitude, "Labour not for the meat which perisheth," recorded also how he was unwilling to send the multitude away unfed lest they should faint by the way. Though Christian Socialism originated with the Broad Church school, it now draws many of its most devoted adherents from the High Church wing. Nonconformity has also given many workers to the Labour party: more than one Labour leader of to-day began as a Nonconformist preacher. That is one of the things which cause the British Labour Party to appear contemptible in the eyes of Continental Socialists.

One great line of Christian activity in the world cannot be dealt with in the compass of this volume, the propagation of Christianity in non-Christian countries by Roman Catholic, Anglican and Protestant missionaries. The nineteenth century saw the great development of Anglican and Protestant missions. This particular subject may here be left undiscussed with the better reason that there is another volume of this series specially devoted to it.[1] One quotation only may here be given from a German scholar, a recognized authority in the field of primitive Christianity:

> "The advances of Christianity in its early days were small and slow compared with its recent growth and the work of modern missions. The most signal expansion of Christianity belongs not to the first, but to the nineteenth, century."—(H. Weinel, *Die urchristliche und die heutige Mission.* Tübingen, 1907.)

We have brought our rapid survey of Christianity, as an element in the world of men, down to the present day. If the claim is made for the Christian society that it embodies a new supernatural life, which would necessarily show itself in a type of conduct above that of ordinary men, the sins and errors and failures

[1] *Missions: their Rise and Development*, by Mrs. Creighton.

which mark the story of the Christian Church might seem to dispose of that claim once for all. If a Christian can substantiate it, it cannot be by his denying the sins and errors and failures, but by the view that the new life is something which, in the Purpose of God, prevails only gradually over the crude material of human nature. Christianity has not failed: it has still only very partially subdued men to itself—which is an altogether different thing. In spite of all that is defective in the conduct of those who call themselves Christians, there may be seen in every age the persistent inner life of the great tree which has sprung from the little seed of the Kingdom flowering in lives of a peculiar quality which, in all individual variations, can be called distinctively Christian. And if the periods of general declension have to be noted, what is perhaps the most notable thing in the story is the way in which over and over again some Power working in the Body seems to emerge, to revivify what is dying and restore what is decayed—a power of reparation, coming not from outside, but from within the Body itself, its emergence meaning in one way a new advance, but in another way always a return of the Christian community for fresh inspiration to the original source of its life.

CHAPTER XI

THE SITUATION TO-DAY

In this concluding chapter we have to consider the position of Christianity in the modern world, and the conditions under which anyone has to decide for or against it. Do present facts indicate that the Christian faith is likely or not to be abandoned by Europeans? No doubt people are apt to interpret the signs favourably to their own system of belief about the Universe; yet the truth of Christianity does not really imply the impossibility of Europe's becoming pagan, nor the falsehood of Christianity the impossibility of Europe's being on the eve of a great revival of Christian religion. What makes it difficult to predict from present facts is that the chief characteristic of the religious situation in present-day Europe is confusion. In former times belief and disbelief in Christianity were much more sharply marked off in white and black: there were believers, and there were people called "infidels," and you could roughly see which predominated. To-day an endless variety of forms of belief are jumbled up together. There are few educated Christians who do not now admit things which were once asserted against Christianity by "infidels" and few educated disbelievers in Christianity who have not discarded some of the things which "infidels" used to assert.

One can see large masses of men in every European country who have abandoned the practice of any religion and follow various kinds of pleasure: perhaps thousands of people spend Sunday flying about in cars who, if conditions were as they were a hundred years ago, would go to church. But this kind of mass-drifting away from formal religion is not really much indication as to the future prospects of Christianity. It comes partly from a rapid increase in recent times of the material means of pleasure. The great bulk of people who fly about in cars are not people who have seriously considered alternative views of the world and abandoned Christianity because they have found it unsatisfactory to their best selves: they simply follow the impulse of the moment to enjoy without considering any view of the world seriously at all. In the long run the beliefs prevalent in society are determined by those members of it who do consider the problems of life and the world seriously: any view on which a considerable body of systematic inquirers in science or philosophy agree spreads, sooner or later, with various degrees of popular simplification or misunderstanding, through the community at large. But if we remove from consideration the great mass of merely thoughtless people, and limit our view to the minority who choose or reject Christianity because, on an adequate knowledge of the facts of the world, they find themselves drawn one way or the other, it is still very difficult to get a sure basis for prognostication. Obviously those who do prognosticate are liable to a particular kind of illusion, arising from their own immediate environment. An anti-Christian teacher in a University or an anti-Christian man of letters will naturally draw round him a group of young men to whom his view of life is congenial, and is likely to generalize from these about the rising generation as a whole: a Christian leader of personality and influence will come in contact with a large number of young men of another sort, and declare perhaps that the signs of a vigorous Christianity in the coming days are very encouraging.

It would be the surest indication of a proximate desertion of Christianity if, when we looked at the men who are acknowledged to stand high in the understanding of modern thought and modern science, we discovered no Christians amongst them. We should then be able to assert, with facts to confirm our assertion, that belief in Christianity was incompatible with modern knowledge. What however we do see, when we look, is something quite different. Some forms of Christianity it would be difficult to find amongst those of the first rank, as philosophers and scientists—the "Fundamentalism" which believes that the early chapters of Genesis are literal history. It would be difficult, on the other hand, to find many modern philosophers who maintain the old materialism. Marxists still apparently hold to it, being Fundamentalists the other way round, who believe in the infallibility of Karl Marx. But a number of forms of Christianity are represented amongst men of the first rank side by side with men who hold various views of the universe irreconcilable with Christianity. We can find Anglicans and Roman Catholics and Quakers and members of the various "Free Churches." This state of things proves that the most extensive knowledge of modern science and understanding of modern thought neither compels a man to be a Christian, nor is incompatible with his being one. It certainly proves that to speak as if the controversy between Christianity and non-Christian views of the world had been decided by consensus in Europe against Christianity is premature.

In the last chapter something was said about the drift to Unitarianism, veiled or avowed. We see to-day a tendency widely at work, both within the Protestant churches and outside the churches altogether—the tendency to imagine a form of religion which, it is thought, would still be distinctively Christian and at the same time acceptable to the "modern man." Such a religion would throw off all traditional Christian belief about a descent and self-humiliation of God, in the coming and the dying of Jesus Christ, and hold up simply the human figure of Jesus or the "values" enunciated by Jesus, extracted from the Gospel record, as sufficient basis for a religion by which for all time men could go on calling themselves Christians. There is a particular phrase much in favour to-day because it is a convenient screen behind which the substitution of a merely human Jesus for the Christ of Christian faith may be effected without the operation becoming too apparent. The significance of Jesus is stated by saying that he by his personality "revealed God"—"God is like Jesus." No Christian would question that this is an important truth about Jesus: it is insisted upon in the New Testament—"He that hath seen me hath seen the Father." But when it is given as the most sufficient brief statement of what the Divinity of Jesus means, what his principal work was, it conceals a grave ambiguity. For every good man in his measure reveals God: indeed there is no creature which does not in some sense show what God is like. A mirror reveals an object without being the object. A great action, on the other hand, reveals the character of the agent by being itself the agent in operation. According to the Christian faith, Jesus revealed God in the latter sense, not in the way a mirror reveals: in Jesus God did His supreme act of love for men. The phrase is misleading in another way, when used as it commonly is. It implies that the supreme need of men was for more knowledge: if they were shown what goodness was, practically everything required for their salvation was accomplished. Certainly, according to the Christian faith, men did need more knowledge, they did need to have a clearer idea of what goodness was, but they needed a great deal besides. By knowing what goodness is men do not necessarily become good. The Son of God, according to the original Gospel, came to do something much more than extend men's knowledge, even than extend their knowledge of God.

The way of bringing Christianity up to date just spoken of may appear at first sight very simple and attractive, yet, whatever is going to happen, it seems safe to predict that this way at any rate has no future. It is certain indeed that the figure of Jesus, if all Christian belief were given up, would always remain a figure in human history exceedingly beautiful, pathetic and impressive, that it would continue to act as a stimulus to men's spiritual life, as all beautiful things do, and that many of the detached sayings of Jesus would continue current as the expression of profound moral truths. But the figure would have limitations which made it unreasonable for men to go on calling themselves after this one man for all time. He would only be one in a class with the Buddha, Socrates, Plato, Epictetus, with the great poets and with those who have suffered, because of their goodness, the hatred and cruelty of men.

A wide range of human values, cultural and intellectual, lay wholly outside the earthly horizon of Jesus of Nazareth. Many of his sayings about God and man, charming as they are, would then have a *naïveté* which disqualified them from giving serious guidance to men who have maturer knowledge of the world. Other sayings of his, such as that in which he bids men *fear* God who " is able to destroy both soul and body in hell " are not at all to the taste of the modern man and have to be got out of sight when a picture of Jesus is composed sympathetic to the wide-minded charity of our own time. And as a figure calculated to inspire men to heroic acts of self-sacrifice, it may be doubted whether the figure of Jesus, if detached from what Christians have believed about him, is adequate. There are sayings of his which bid men give up everything for the Kingdom of Heaven's sake, but his own life, unless what Christians have believed is true, does not offer any signal example of self-sacrifice. Mr. Claude Montefiore has observed, very pertinently on his premisses, that while Jesus laid down as a precept that men should love their enemies, there is no recorded instance of his showing love to Pharisees.[1] Mr. Montefiore might have carried his observation further; there is no recorded instance of Jesus showing love to publicans and sinners at great cost to himself. He ate and drank with them indeed, but, for

[1] " What one would have wished to find in the life-story of Jesus would be one single incident in which Jesus actually performed a loving deed to one of his Rabbinic antagonists or enemies. That would have been worth all the *injunctions* of the Sermon on the Mount about the love of enemies put together."—*Rabbinic Literature and Gospel Teachings* (Macmillan, 1930), p. 104.

that matter, he is also said on more than one occasion to have eaten and drunk with Pharisees. A wandering life in Palestine is not a life of luxury, but it is a very much pleasanter life than that lived by millions to-day in our great cities. There is the Cross. Yes, but, apart from the belief of the Church, it must be exceedingly doubtful whether Jesus incurred the suffering of the Cross voluntarily, with prevision of the destiny to which his action was leading. The predictions of his death put into his mouth in the Gospels cannot, if you rule out the supernatural, ever have been uttered by him in the form given; and they may have been invented *de toutes pièces* for obvious reasons in the primitive Nazoræan community. It is impossible to disprove the theory that when Jesus came to Jerusalem and began to take high-handed action in the Temple, which he knew must bring him into collision with the authorities, he was convinced that at the critical moment God would intervene on his behalf with overwhelming power and bring in the Kingdom of heaven. The dreadful cry upon the Cross can be understood to mean that his crucifixion was an appalling surprise to him. The last word of the great Teacher in our earliest Gospel would then proclaim his ultimate discovery that the beautiful idea of the loving Father in heaven, on which all his teaching had been built, did not fit the hideous facts of the real world.

Of course, if what Christians, from the time of our earliest documents, have believed about

Jesus is true, none of these limitations impair the Figure. If Jesus dealt in the most perfect way possible with the matter supplied by his environment during those few years of his earthly life in Palestine, it need not trouble us that the matter was narrow in range, for, according to the belief of the Church, the whole compass of human interests is to be brought into harmony by the operation, throughout the ages, of a Spirit who is the Spirit of Jesus himself in his community, a community potentially coextensive with man. Again, the sayings about God which must seem so childishly *naïf*, if they were said about a God who did not "so love the world," may be simple truth if they were said about the God who came down to win the hearts of men in the Person of the Divine Being one with Himself. Yet again, if Jesus was indeed this Divine Being come down, the whole of his earthly life was an act of infinite self-sacrifice; it is unquestionable then that its consummation, the supreme sacrifice of the Cross, was voluntary, and that Jesus died for Saul the Pharisee every bit as much as for Matthew the publican. "The Son of God who loved me and gave himself for me"—it was one of his Rabbinic enemies who said that. It was the very Pharisee who is accused of having obscured the simple teaching of Jesus by his theological theory. Yet his seeing in the death upon the Cross an act of love in which he individually was embraced was a delusion unless his theological theory was the truth.

What makes the proposal to have a modernized Christianity based upon the human Figure of Jesus alone, apart from "theological dogma" seem so plausible, is that the Figure has acquired a power of appeal, as embodying the supreme ideal of self-sacrificing love, just because the belief of the Church in regard to Jesus was presupposed. By old association the Figure can still have that power of appeal for a time, even when the belief of the Church about it has been given up. The name of Jesus has a traditional suggestion about it, a halo which subjugates men's minds. But if the ground on which that suggestion, that halo, became first attached to the name is gone, the glamour sooner or later must fade, and men must recognize the truth in the light of common day—that at the source of Christianity in Palestine there was a very remarkable and attractive personality of some kind, but that all imaginative reconstructions of that personality based upon our fragmentary data must be highly conjectural.

All this does not exclude the possibility that Unitarianism in a wider sense, a monotheistic religion not tied in any peculiar way to the one figure of Jesus, might become the predominant religion of Europe. Such a religion, however, could not legitimately call itself Christianity, except perhaps in the sense of being continuous, in some of its religious and ethical standards, with the Christian Europe of former centuries. And it should be noted that such a monotheism, not specifically Christian, would almost inevitably take one or other of two lines. On the one hand the idea of God might be that of a transcendent Person, Creator and Ruler of the world, as in Judaism and Islam. Then, since He would no longer be a God who had so loved the world that He had entered Himself into its history in the way in which Christians believe Him to have done, His being, in His sovereign separateness above the world, would be altogether problematic, would be simply inscrutable Power. The physical universe, taken by itself, could not be said to prove a God of love or a God of goodness. Judaism, it is true, though it thinks of God as transcendent, thinks of Him also with a warm familiarity, but that is just because it thinks of Him as doing definite acts, choosing definite people, in human history, and so begins the thought of God which Christianity has carried on. It does not, however, seem likely that a Europe which had abandoned the belief that God came down in Jesus Christ would adhere to the belief that God called Abraham. With a God transcendent in the way described, the problem of the world's evil would become much more grievous. What reason would there be to think that the Unknown Person throned above the world had any care for the pain of man, for the struggle of goodness ?

On the other hand, the new religion might take the line of conceiving God as immanent in the whole world-process. This would no doubt in a way bring Him near. But His personality would inevitably become blurred, and, with His personality, His character. There would be no events, no human persons, wherein He manifested Himself in a special way, because He would be indistinguishably in all events and all persons. It would be difficult to see any goal, any meaning, in the world-process. The meaning of the word "God" itself would become obscure, or connote simply a kind of feeling which a man had when he contemplated the Universe as a whole, the feeling of being up against something very big. A man might indeed, from studying the Universe, come to the conclusion that something analogous to the human mind was at work in it, something like the Supreme Mathematician of Sir James Jeans, but the Mathematician might be as indifferent to all moral values, to human pain and human conflict, as the curiously contriving mind of ants and bees.

It will be seen that Christianity does not follow either of the two ways stated. It has taken over from Judaism belief in a God who is a Person distinct from the world, Creator and Ruler of the world, but not a God separate from the world, as a purely transcendent God would be. For Christianity has also taken over from Judaism the belief that God does definite things in the world-process, chooses persons and peoples for definite purposes, guides the whole process to an end already adumbrated in the Divine Community. Its distinctive belief is that God in the Person of a particular Man entered Himself into the suffering of humanity, and planted within humanity, in the Divine Community, the seed of a new supernatural life. God, so conceived, is transcendent, above the world, but not aloof, not indifferent to the world; God is present in the world, but not revealed with equal fullness and purity in a jelly-fish and in a man, in a vicious man and in a good man, in all other good men and in Jesus.

At present there is no other religion in Europe, beside Christianity, which commands the allegiance of any considerable body of men—Judaism is practically confined to a single race which must always be very much in a minority. There are, of course, large numbers of people who reject Christianity. But the mass of people outside Christianity do not form any united body on the basis of an alternative view of the universe shared by all. There is merely a babel of numberless different beliefs. It is quite an illusion to suppose that there is such a thing as a "scientific" view of the Universe alternative to Christianity. Men of science are very largely in agreement where the facts and laws of the physical world are in question; but when the specifically religious question is raised, whether the facts and laws of the physical world are compatible with the reality of a spiritual world behind or within the physical world, and, if there is a spiritual world, what its nature is, "Science" as such cannot pronounce, and the views of men of science fly apart any number of different ways, just as the views of ordinary men do. Most of the talk about the inevitable "conflict between Science and Religion" comes from a desire to deal in philosophic generalizations with no sufficient attention to the distinction between what is essential and what is accidental in the conflicts of the past. There can be a conflict between Science and Religion only when Religion implies the assertion of facts in the field accessible to scientific observation. This was the case when Religion asserted the truth of the Ptolemaic astronomy against Galileo, or the literal truth of Genesis i and Genesis ii (which, of course, are not in agreement with each other) against the geologists and Darwin.

The men of to-day have then to choose between one of the forms of Christianity or some form of non-Christian belief followed by a group in the confusion outside Christianity. And, as has been pointed out, some non-Christian groups adopt so many Christian elements, and some groups claiming to be Christian give up so much of traditional Christian belief, that it may be hard to say precisely where the division between Christian and non-Christian now comes. Among the most curious groups is that whose chief exponent is a French scholar, Dr. P. L. Couchoud: it sees a high value in Pauline theology as a beautiful myth enshrining spiritual truths, but maintains that no person who ever really existed can be discerned through the Gospel picture of Jesus. One thing seems plain. Each form of belief presents itself as a systematic whole, and a man who deliberately and thoughtfully chooses, as his hypothesis to live by, any one of them, does so because his nature as a whole, his mind and feeling and sense of worth, responds to its appeal. His choice is not determined simply by the conclusion of a process of reasoning which he is able to set forth in words, but by something much larger and deeper. It is this which makes it so futile to suppose that you can by any short knock-down argument prove or disprove any of the systems of belief, Christian or anti-Christian, to which men fully equipped with modern knowledge of the world adhere. One has only to look at any controversial correspondence in the Press between Christians and non-Christians to see the absurd reliance placed by correspondents on some argument—say, the play made by anti-Christians with such terms as "rational" or "anthropomorphic"—which the other side has long ago considered, and to which it has ready an answer held satisfactory by some men eminently reasonable and well-informed.

If a man chooses Roman Catholicism or some other form of Christianity or some atheistic theory of the world, he does so because, confronted with that view of the world as a whole, he feels in himself that this view is the best. The only way therefore by which you can judge of any Christian, or non-Christian, view of the world is to consider how it is set forth as a complete system by its best representatives, and the most effectual way in which acceptance can be won for a true system of belief is its being set as completely as possible before the minds of men. If we take present-day forms of Christian belief, which do not, like belief in the literal truth of the Mosaic cosmogony, conflict with ascertained facts of the world, attack on them usually takes the form of showing that they do not follow with logical necessity from admitted premisses: the finger is laid on points where the argument for them is logically inconclusive. The charge is perfectly true: the argument for them *is* logically inconclusive. Only it has also to be recognized that the argument for any non-Christian view of the world is logically inconclusive. There is no religious (or anti-religious) view of the Universe which can be demonstrated with logical necessity from generally admitted premisses. Whatever hypothesis regarding the Ground of the Universe a man adopts, he makes a leap beyond experience. He is compelled to make the leap by the necessity of living. If we were only spectators of reality we could practise complete suspension of judgment till we saw what happened. But we are, by our voluntary acts, makers all the time of new reality, and we cannot make new reality without acting on some hypothesis regarding the nature of the Universe in which we act. It might be supposed that the attitude of Agnostics, being non-committal, saves them from the risk of an option. Of course, it does not. With regard to the character of a man in a story I may suspend my judgment till the course of the story shows whether he is good or bad; but if I am in practical daily contact with a man I have to act either on the hypothesis that he is trustworthy or that he is not: to suspend my judgment is in effect to decide that I am not going to trust him. If I trust him, I run the risk of finding in the end that I was taken in: but also if I do not trust him, I run the risk of finding that I have missed the good which intercourse with a fellow-man might have procured. We are in practical daily contact with the Universe. Christians, who act on the hypothesis that behind the Universe is a Power who loves men and cares for goodness may prove to have been mistaken; but Agnostics, who decide not to trust the Universe so far, may also prove to have been mistaken and to have missed the true significance of human life on this planet.

If to be an Agnostic is to acknowledge that the hypothesis on which one acts is a matter of faith and not of knowledge, all discerning Christians are Agnostics.[1] But Agnosticism ordinarily means acting on the hypothesis that the Christian faith is not true—equally with Christianity a leap beyond experience. If men choose to live by the Christian faith, it is because the Christian faith, in one of its varieties, seems to them the worthiest hypothesis to live by. Whether a life lived according to the Christian ideal is or is not the best kind of life is a question which each individual can decide only by an intuitive judg-

[1] We have but faith, we cannot know,
For knowledge is of things we see.—(TENNYSON.)
We walk by faith, and not by sight.—(ST. PAUL.)

ment or perception, just as men decide whether a work of art is beautiful or not. But a man might be convinced that the Christian life was the life of highest spiritual value without having the Christian faith. For faith means the belief that existence corresponds to value: it is conceivable that the spiritual ideals which man has might be something merely in the mind of man, and the great Universe all round might be wholly indifferent to them. Recognition of value is a matter of immediate intuition, but the belief that the Universe in its ultimate ground *is* good is the leap of faith. There is no argument which can prove a work of art to be beautiful to anyone who does not see it as beautiful, and no argument which can prove the Christian ideal for life to be best to the person who does not see it as best: also there is no argument which can compel anyone to make the leap of faith. To some men, however, it seems so immediately clear that the Christian ideal for life is the best, and they have so strong a conviction that existence corresponds to value, that they hold the Christian faith with as full an assurance as if they held it as a necessary logical conclusion from indubitable premisses. Further, the experiences of their lives, the way they are directed by outside circumstances, the inner experiences of evil checked, strength renewed, light enlarged, seem to them as surely the working of Someone else, of God, as the words and actions of their fellow-men are the manifestation of other persons with whom they have to do. Such experiences can have small evidential value for any-one else, unless he has had similar experiences of his own : if described to another person, they can always be plausibly explained according to some supposed psychological law. But for the man who sees the things which happen to him and the things which happen within him as the work of God, the conviction that they are the work of God may be continually confirmed. His faith, though it remains faith, and is not demonstration, may come to have for him a certainty which leaves no room for doubt. Of course, in the majority of Christian lives faith does not reach this complete assurance, but shows all degrees of wavering and intermittence. The test is not how far a man can logically analyse his reasons for believing, but how far in practice he will stake his life on his belief. The typical assertor of Christianity is the martyr —the "witness" in that way. And though few of us now are confronted with the alternative of denying the Christian faith or being killed, the demand to stake life upon the hypothesis of faith comes in other ways to all Christians, it may be in some great sacrifice, it may be in the continual small sacrifices of every day.

It is only as he looks at each Christian, and at each non-Christian, view of the world as a whole that a man can reasonably judge it. Whichever view he chooses as best satisfying his intellect, his sense of values, his essential self, he must necessarily reject the others. But he should recognize that several of those others can be held by men as intelligent, as rational, as well-informed regarding the facts of the world as himself. His exposition of the grounds on which he rejects each of them can, if he is honest, only take the form of an analysis of his own reaction to them—at this or the other point he personally feels that they are unsatisfactory to his moral feeling, or are arbitrary, or offer a construction of the facts of the world which seems to him improbable. But if he thinks to bowl them out by convicting those who hold them of some obvious absurdity, it will probably be a mark of his own shallowness.

It may here be objected that, even if it be true that all hypotheses regarding the ultimate Ground of the Universe, Christian and non-Christian alike, are leaps beyond experience, no reason has been shown why men should leap in the Christian direction rather than in any other. That is true. To set forth why men may reasonably make such a choice is to offer a philosophical defence for Christian faith, and to do that lies outside the scope of this little volume. But if anyone wants to know how those men who, equipped with such knowledge of the world as scientific research and philosophic thought have reached to-day, have given their adherence to a Christian view of the world, justify their choice at the bar of reason, he has only to attend to what those men themselves have to say. While for some forms of Christianity, as has been said, it would be difficult to-day to find philosophic defenders of the first rank, for other forms there is no lack of them. What, however, strikes one about most contemporary attacks on Christian views of the world is how seldom they come to close quarters with any Christian view as set forth by its best exponents. They do not, as a rule, grapple with the Roman Catholic view set forth by Baron Friedrich von Hügel or by Jacques Maritain or Father M. C. D'Arcy, or with the Anglican view set forth by William Temple or Charles Gore or Percy Gardner or Clement Webb or A. E. Taylor or W. R. Matthews or F. R. Tennant, or the Presbyterian view set forth by D. S. Cairns or George Galloway or J. Y. Simpson, or the Congregational view set forth by A. E. Garvie or W. B. Selbie. They almost always attack Christianity as they have found it represented by some poorly-educated clergyman in the next street, or some dull traditionalist who taught them at school. This is quite in accordance with the precept of good Sir Thomas Browne, who advises us that "to confirm and establish our opinions, 'tis best to argue with judgments below our own, that the frequent spoils and Victories over their reasons may settle in ourselves an esteem and confirmed Opinion of our own." By attacking Christianity in its most ignorant exponents, or even grossly caricaturing it after their own fancy, as a preparation for overthrowing it, they are able to arrive at the little chirrup of felt intellectual superiority far more easily than if they had to address themselves to a system of thought set forth by a competent and able contemporary thinker.

It is probably true that philosophic defences of belief—all that is included under the term Apologetics—have seldom, if ever, given a man the impulse to believe. The most they can do is to help where the impulse to believe is there, but is thwarted and neutralized by an apparent conflict between belief and a rational view of the facts of the world. In such cases Christian philosophy may put before a man a view of the world which does justice to the facts and at the same time makes the leap of faith appear to him reasonable. But the impulse to believe itself must come, if it comes at all, from the direct perception that a particular kind of life is the life most worth living. For those who have it the perception is a supernatural call—which, according as they will, they may follow or they may refuse.

INDEX

INDEX